Exploring and Applying the Lord's Prayer

A prayer to change the world

John Belham

PARVA PRESS

Copyright © 2022 by John Belham

The right of the author has been asserted.
All rights reserved. No part of this publication may be reproduced, distributed or transmitted in any form or by any means, without prior written permission.

Parva Press
Web: https://lords-prayer.co.uk
E-mail: parvapress@lords-prayer.co.uk

This book is a revised and updated edition of the paperback first published by Parva Press in 200 under the title, *Lord teach us to pray . . . The Lord's Prayer explored and applied* ISBN 0-9537489-0-1

The Bible quotations, paraphrases and allusions are taken from The Holy Bible Authorised King James Version.

British Library Cataloguing in Publication Data
A catalogue record for this publication is available from the British Library.

Book Layout © 2017 BookDesignTemplates.com

Exploring and Applying the Lord's Prayer
A prayer to change the world
John Belham

ISBN 978-0-9537489-4-5

To the glory of God
and for the encouragement of his people

An English text of the prayer itself

> Our Father in heaven,
> Hallowed be your name.
> Your kingdom come.
> Your will be done on earth, as it is in heaven.
> Give us this day our daily bread.
>   And forgive us our trespasses,
>   as we forgive those who trespass against us.
>   And lead us not into temptation,
>   but deliver us from evil;
>   For yours is the kingdom, the power
>   and the glory for ever. Amen

CONTENTS

An Invitation 1
Our Father in Heaven 3
    The gracious encounter 3
Hallowed be Your Name 9
    Worship, but not only with our lips 9
Your Kingdom Come 19
    The King and his domain 19
Your Will be Done 29
    Godly living and dying 29
Your Will be Done, continued 35
    The great principle of godly government 35
As it is in Heaven 43
    A shaft of sunlight 43
Give us Today our Daily Bread 53
    Strength and freedom to live 53
Forgive us our Trespasses 63
    A fresh clean start 63
Forgive us our Trespasses, continued 71
    Ongoing, day by day forgiveness 71
As we Forgive those who Trespass against us 77
    Eager and ready to forgive 77
Lead us not into Temptation 87
    Surrounded by so many dangers 87

Keep us, Deliver us from Evil 97
   Safety in an evil world.. 97
Deliver us from Evil, continued 109
   The one who would deceive and destroy.................................. 109
The Kingdom, the Power and the Glory...................................... 119
   A concluding peal of praise 119
The Whole Prayer in Practical Use.. 125
   The great sweep of human history, or the details of one person or situation 125
The Lord's Prayer Spelled Out... 129
   An extended paraphrase 129
Postscript 131
Acknowledgement 133
   A Greater Acknowledgement 133
The Author and our Other Publications....................................... 137

An Invitation

You are personally invited to spend time as an honoured guest in a great house. You have complete freedom to enjoy the magnificence of the splendid rooms, but also have freedom to visit the more practical rooms – the kitchens, store rooms, even the bathrooms and security rooms. You are free to meet with members of the household, to admire the furnishings, to pause at the windows and enjoy both the lovely gardens and the fine sweeping views across the estate.

Such, and infinitely greater, is the wonderful invitation given to every disciple within the lines of the Lord's Prayer. Rather than a prayer to be repeated, it is more like a magnificent house to explore.

As with a great house, childishness might lead us to rush from room to room without any appreciation of the privilege of the invitation or of the beauty of the rooms and their setting. We would soon find it all too familiar and boring. Sadly, many true Christian folk find the Lord's Prayer to be just that.

However, given patience and a willingness to apply it to each part of our personal and social life, we will be thrilled to discover what a manual for Christian living is contained in these few memorable words.

For those who will accept it with wonder and a humble willingness to learn, the Lord's Prayer is an invitation to be greatly treasured. It will move us to trust, challenge us to give and stir us to worship. It will show us the depths of our unforgiving hearts and teach us to walk warily. Above all, it will open our eyes to see what it is to live with a single aim of bringing glory to our heavenly Father.

Our Father in Heaven

The gracious encounter

The Lord's Prayer is recorded in the gospels of both Matthew and Luke. In Matthew, it forms a part of the Sermon on the Mount. In Luke, the disciples had been with Jesus for many months. They had heard him speak and seen him heal the sick and set men free. They had also seen their Lord rise a great while before daybreak to be quiet; to spend time alone with his heavenly Father.

Luke tells us that Jesus had just returned from such a time of prayer, and so it was natural for them to ask, 'Lord, teach us to pray.' As a result of that request we have what we call 'The Lord's Prayer'. The prayer is our Lord's teaching and our Lord's pattern concerning prayer. It is how we should pray.

The Lord's Prayer was not given as a literary masterpiece to be viewed and admired. Nor is it a beautiful set piece to be recited morning by morning as if the lovely words themselves would infuse a beauty into our lives but had no practical meaning or bearing on the way we live. It was given to be a pattern and a basis of prayer for real people in the real world. It is the pattern our Lord has given his disciples. Even then it is not only a recitation or set prayer but truly a whole house of prayer with many rooms to explore. Each phrase of the prayer or 'room' opens to us a different aspect of God's world, the world for which we are called to pray.

Beware then, of rushing around the house from phrase to phrase, room to room simply 'checking them off'. But rather, take time to walk from room to room, phrase to phrase, and bring before our heavenly Father, the people, the contents and the views, both near and far, of each room or phrase in turn.

We begin with just the first phrase, 'Our Father in heaven,' or, 'Father,' as it is in the earliest copies of Luke's gospel. Here is the grand entrance hall in which we are introduced to the King. Our Lord teaches us straight away to whom we should pray and, indeed, who may pray in this way.

The Lord was teaching his Hebrew disciples to pray, and the Hebrew people were very proud of Abraham their father. Abraham was the friend of God. Abraham was successful in pleading with God to spare cities. It would have been quite natural, from our point of view at least, for our Lord to have taught them to pray: 'Father Abraham, friend of God, plead for us, pray for us.' But he did not do that.

There were other great spiritual leaders, for example Moses. When God spoke with ordinary men, he spoke with them from a distance, but when God spoke with Moses he spoke with him face to face. So it would have been natural, again from our point of view, if our Lord had said, 'Pray like this: "Father Moses, to whom has been given the privilege of speaking with God face to face, pray for us, intercede for us, pray on our behalf."' But again, he did not. The same of Elijah, that great man of God by whose passionate prayers came drought, fire and rain: 'Elijah pray for us; intercede on our behalf.'

Our Lord nowhere teaches us to pray in this way and neither do his chosen apostles, and there is an enormous lesson here straight away. If we would be disciples of our Lord Jesus: if we are willing to submit to his teaching, we will not offer our prayers to those Old Testament saints or to their New Testament counterparts.

In this prayer our Lord offers us a privilege far, far greater. We are not invited to come to a mere servant of God, no matter how great a spiritual giant he or she may have been. We are invited to come with boldness into the very presence of the God and Father of our Lord Jesus Christ; invited to speak with Almighty God himself.

The invitation is absolutely overwhelming. How dare we? We certainly may not by any merit or right of our own. But, through his Son, the Lord God invites us, as we pray, to come into his awesome and royal presence; indeed, we are called to do so with boldness, and by express invitation.

Once we have understood the greatness and amazing privilege of such an invitation, to refuse would be as unthinkably rude as receiving an invitation to a royal reception or garden party but, on the occasion, actively choosing to speak only with the servants.

How should we address Almighty God?
We are taught to approach him as 'our Father in heaven'. This again is something absolutely wonderful; that we, mere mortals, are invited to address the sovereign Lord of the entire universe as, 'Father'. The Hebrew people of our Lord's day knew almost nothing of this intimate knowledge of God. And in our own day and culture, for a variety of reasons, many people find it very difficult. We think more easily of God as an impersonal cosmic force, or the 'great architect', or maybe the pattern set by our own father is a great stumbling block. However, the privilege of Christ's disciples is that we may know God, the Sovereign Lord, as our heavenly Father; the best and greatest of Fathers, who loves us and cares for us.

The apostle Paul puts it even more strongly when he says that those who have the Spirit of our Lord Jesus can address God the creator as 'Abba', 'Father, my Father'. That is the privilege of disciples of our Lord Jesus. We can, in a real sense, be sons and daughters with the freedom of approach seen in a little child with a loving parent.

Who may pray like this?
Here is a prayer for disciples of our Lord Jesus. He came to his own people, writes the apostle John, and they did not receive him. They rejected him. But to those among them who received him he gave the power, the right, the authority to be the sons and daughters of God.

Those in our own day who are given this right and privilege, are also those who receive the Lord Jesus; those who are willing to trust him for who he is and for what he has done for us; willing to learn what he commands and willing to do it. These, and only these, are true disciples of Christ and to them is given this great and glorious privilege – to be the sons and daughters of God.

Finally, do notice that this is the family prayer; a prayer for all disciples. So, rightly, in English the prayer begins with the little word our; not just my Father but our Father. The one who hears equally the cries of the strong man or the little child, the prince in his palace or the poor man cast out. He, our Father, hears the cry of the prisoner as clearly as the cry of the free, the prayers of the despised as gladly as the prayers of those held in high public esteem.

True disciples of the Lord Jesus, no matter what their earthly circumstances, are no more, and no less, than sons and daughters of the living God. We are invited to come with equal boldness, and with equal humility, as brothers and sisters into the very presence of God. The squire and the stable hand, the president and the plumber, the carpenter and the king, disciples met behind cottage doors or cathedral doors – 'our Father'.

Here, truly, is common prayer, a prayer common to disciples from every nation, tongue and tribe, a prayer for the smallest child and a prayer for the strongest leader, a prayer for those who have the responsibility of great power and wealth – and for fellow disciples who do not even know whether there will be a next meal.

When we truly begin to grasp that our fellow disciples, no matter what their earthly circumstances may be, are our brothers and sisters in Christ, it will begin to move our hearts with God-like compassion as it challenges us to give and forgive, to share and to care for those around us.

In beginning to pray the Lord's Prayer, pray just this first line, 'Our Father in heaven,' and then, before moving on, pause and reflect into whose presence we are invited to come with such boldness. Step back and in wonder reflect that we may speak with the Lord God himself. Recall at what cost that privilege was bought; reflect with the apostle Paul that, '. . . the Son of God loved me and gave himself for me.'

If you pause and consider these things you may well be moved to worship, and moved in wonder and love for God who gave his only Son for you. Filled with awe and wonder, prayer begins to come alive; prayer to our Father in heaven who cares passionately about this world and its people; who cares enough about us to make us his children.

'Father, give us a due sense of awe and wonder at the greatness of this your invitation. Set our hearts ablaze in wonder and thanksgiving that in your unchanging love and mercy you gave your Son, your only Son, that we, together, might be sons and daughters of the living God.'

Questions

These questions are offered simply as an optional help for personal reflection or group discussion.

1. How do you respond to the suggestion that the Lord's Prayer is more than a prayer to recite; it is also a prayer to explore and apply phrase by phrase?
2. Do you find it rather surprising that our Lord did not teach us to pray to, or through, the great servants of God?
3. Can you sense the wonder and privilege of addressing almighty God as 'Father'?
4. Who can rightly do so?
5. How can this move us to worship, and bring our prayers to life?
6. What is the significance of the little word 'our'?

References

Given in the order in which they occur in the chapter.
The Lord's Prayer – Matthew 6:9-13 and Luke 11:1-4
Abraham pleading – Genesis 18:22-33
Moses speaking face to face – Exodus 33:9-11
Elijah. Passionate prayer – James 5:17&18
God as 'Abba' – Romans 8:14-17
The right to be the sons and daughters of God – John 1:11&12
We love him, because he first loved us – 1 John 4:19

Hallowed be Your Name

Worship, but not only with our lips

Like a great house, the Lord's Prayer is built around three magnificent central rooms. These are: a passionate concern for the honour of our heavenly Father's name, the extending of his kingdom and the doing of his will. These three great concerns lie at the heart of the prayer and must surely be the concerns of all those who are true disciples.

As the text comes to us in the Greek, each of these first three petitions is short, God-centred, urgent and complete, 'Hallow your name, Bring in your kingdom, Cause your will to be done.' The words reflect and inspire an eagerness to see God's sovereign rule completely and finally established. They look forward to the fulfilment of human history but they also fire our personal thinking and touch our individual lives here and now.

Beginning with just the first of these petitions, when we pray, 'Hallowed be your name,' or, 'Cause your name to be held high, honoured,' what do we mean? We know the line so well and recite it so easily, and yet do we really appreciate the weight and significance of these simple words?

Three questions may help to show the richness of their meaning:

Firstly: Why should we want to see our heavenly Father's name honoured?

Whose name is it we should long to see held in awe? It is not the bare word 'God' itself, used too easily when people find that they have forgotten something, or hit their thumb with a hammer! Nor are we taught to honour a god of our own picturing, such as 'the God of love' or 'the great designer.' Rather, we are taught to honour the God and Father of our Lord Jesus Christ, whose magnificence is seen in the universe and whose character is revealed in scripture. He is the great 'I am' who was and is and always will be Lord and King, Redeemer and Judge.

He brought us into existence
In biblical shorthand, our heavenly Father is maker or creator of the whole universe. Such an understanding does not bind us to any narrow or rigid human theory but does affirm that our heavenly Father is author of all and Lord of all. Our seemingly godless world – with all its exploitation and suffering – is still his world. He is in control of nations, governments and societies. On a personal level, our circumstances, our life, our future, this next week, are all in his hands. Whether we choose to acknowledge it or not, he is the one who has our very breath in his hand. Should not then his name be honoured; held in awe?

We are answerable to him
As author and maker, our heavenly Father has every right to determine how we, his creatures, should live and should behave. Through his chosen spokesmen he has given us very full guidelines for living. He has also warned us that he will call us to account for

the life he has entrusted to us. The Bible describes him as judge. Our words and our deeds, both open and secret, good and evil, are known to him. We shall be called to account for those evil things which we deliberately do and also for that steady rebellion which just ignores him, chooses not to do his will and so fails to honour him. The charge laid before Belshazzar, the ancient king of Babylon, on the night of his death was simply this, 'The God in whose hand is your breath, and all your ways, you have failed to honour.'

At great cost he made possible our rescue
The Lord is the creator, the judge and also, wonderfully, our redeemer. Our heavenly Father cares about this world, cares about each one of us, enough to pay the price for our rescue. He gave his one and only Son so that those who believe will not be swept away in judgment and banished from his sight, but might each be made acceptable before him, given a fresh new start and made a child of God. Here and now his redeemed people have this vital relationship with their heavenly Father; a relationship that not even death can snatch away.

God is the creator, the judge and the saviour. Should not then his wonderful name be held high?

In Stuart Hine's words:
Then sings my soul, my Saviour God, to Thee,
How great Thou art! How great Thou art!

Of course, if it can be proved that God is in no sense author or creator, then it follows that he has no right to tell us how to live or to call us to account for the style of life we choose. It also follows that there is no need of a rescuer or redeemer to put us right with him. Hence the great assault by godless men on the concept of God as creator. However, despite our unthinking or wilful turning our back on God, our heavenly Father remains on the throne. He is creator, judge and redeemer and it is fundamental to our well-being that his name be held high, honoured.

And so to the second question: What does it mean to 'hallow' or 'honour' the name of our heavenly Father?

If we do not have a high regard for people who live or work in the same place as ourselves, we simply take no notice of them. If we are considering a career move, or marriage, or even just planning a holiday we would not dream of consulting them. We are just not interested in their opinion, let alone their advice or moral judgment. If we do not honour someone, in the sense of holding them in esteem, we do not have to say or do anything, we simply pass them by. We ignore them: neighbour, teacher, husband, wife, work colleague, or parent. We ignore them because we regard their opinion and their advice as irrelevant. In practice, many of us behave just like this towards Almighty God. We ignore him; we fail to honour the God in whose hand is our very breath.

On the other hand, if we have a high regard for someone, when we are considering something, if we are able to, we consult them. We will say, 'Now I wonder what so-and-so would think about this?' or, 'I wonder what so-and-so would advise me to do in this situation?' This is how we honour them and this is how we should honour our heavenly Father. As we come to make great decisions, we should ask, 'I wonder what the Lord God has caused to be written about this?' 'Is there some plain teaching, some instruction, a principle or a warning in the scriptures that would apply to this situation?' This is how to honour him and hold high his name; it involves love, respect and, above all, a longing to please him in all that we do and say.

Naturally enough, if we hold his name in such esteem we will not tread it underfoot in our everyday conversation and habits of speech. We will not use it cheaply as a swear-word nor enjoy hearing others doing so. Rather, it will be natural to tell out the greatness of God and to bring honour to his name by our whole way of speaking and living. How well the proverb puts it, 'Give me neither great wealth nor poverty, lest in wealth I forget you, or in poverty I am driven to steal and so bring dishonour on your name.' We honour or dishonour our heavenly Father not only with our lips, by what we say, but with our entire way of life.

Which leads us to ask thirdly: How and where should his name be honoured?

Honoured in our world
'Let all the world in every corner sing, "My God and King,"' wrote George Herbert. This world's peace ultimately depends on the extent to which our heavenly Father's name is honoured. Here is a call to pray that his name may be honoured throughout the whole world and in particular by its statesmen and leaders. Disciples of the Lord Jesus are called to pray and work that his name might be honoured in the corridors of power. If world leaders and peoples share a common submission to our heavenly Father there is a strong foundation for peace and understanding. Pray that God's name might indeed be hallowed by the great leaders and nations of this world.

Honoured in our own land

The scriptures teach that it is godly living or 'righteousness' that lifts up a nation. It is when our Father's name is honoured that a nation becomes truly great. Historically, there is a very striking link between Britain's standing among the nations and the influence of strong and well-grounded Christian leaders in our nation. Look for yourself and see the historical evidence – for example, the good and godly ways championed by people like Wilberforce and Shaftesbury. If you have such God-fearing men and women in positions of authority and leadership, they will work for just laws and fair dealing both nationally and internationally.

When our Father's name is honoured individuals are valued, the weak are protected, evil, violence and vice are restrained and all that is good is encouraged and supported. These are the Lord God's purposes for those in authority at every level – from Parliament to our own homes. Such world-changing thinking lies at the heart of the Lord's Prayer and it is brought most sharply into focus as we pray, 'Your will be done.'

Honoured in the church at large

What is the church? It is intended to be God's own people, a people called out to live for him. A people who will honour him by the way they speak and in the way they live. But the church in Britain, although holding the form of religion, seems chiefly concerned with self-preservation and ceremony and has largely forgotten this radical call to live totally for God, to seek first the honour of his name. We need to pray that our Father's name might be honoured in his Church, nationally.

Honoured in our own local churches
Locally, we have a great museum very close to the church. Our prayer and determination is that the church building, although it is far more ancient than the museum, may not become a 'museum of Christianity'. We long that it might be the meeting place of a vital community of people who love God, and who live, speak and care in such a way as to be a strength, an encouragement and a challenge to those around us; a community of people who truly bring honour to the name of our heavenly Father.

Honoured in our own lives
If we really pray the Lord's Prayer, our prayers will affect the world, our nation and our church, they will also profoundly affect our own homes and lives. We shall begin to pray, 'Lord God may your name be honoured in my own home, in my own working life, in the way I speak, in the way I behave, in my relationships with those around me.'

These are the areas in our own lives on which we need to reflect as we pray, 'Hallowed be your name.'

As you consider this phrase in the Lord's Prayer, reflect on the day that lies ahead, the people you will meet – those who you naturally like and those who provoke you and whose every word seems calculated to trip you, annoy you or crush you with criticism. 'Lord, you know how my blood pressure rises – may your name be honoured'

Helmut Thielicke, the great German pastor and preacher, tells of a businessman who, moving from file to file, interview to interview, would pause just for a moment between each task, take a deep breath and say, 'Glory be to the Father, the Son and the Holy Spirit, Amen,' and then press on. What was he doing? He was really praying, 'May your name be honoured as I tackle this, or as I see this person.' We do well to learn to follow his example. Even as we sit down to write a letter – 'May your name be honoured,' 'Glory be to the Father . . .'

We are only at the first line! Yet if you would in any way begin to plumb the incredible depth of this prayer, pause, consider and apply the words to the world in which we live and then cry from the heart, 'Hallowed be your name.'

'Lord, teach us to pray and seek the honour of your name in our world, in our country, in our own lives and in the lives of those we love.'

Questions for personal reflection or discussion

1. What three great concerns are said to be the three great 'state rooms' of this prayer? Should they be the chief concerns of each true disciple?
2. Why should our heavenly Father's name be held in awe and in the highest honour?
3. How can we hold his name high?
4. Can you think of a situation where someone has been ignored, treated as if they were not there or did not count?
5. Do we do this to Almighty God?
6. How natural and easy is it to remember the Lord as we make our daily decisions?
7. How does stealing bring dishonour to the name of our heavenly Father? Would cheating, tax evasion, drunkenness or reckless driving do the same?

References

'The Judge of all the earth' – Genesis 18:23-25
'The God in whose hand is our breath' – Daniel 5:22&23
The Lord our Redeemer – Galatians 4:4&5, John 3:16 etc.
'Give me not great wealth or poverty' – Proverbs 30:8&9
Righteousness and greatness – Proverbs 14:34

Your Kingdom Come

The King and his domain

By royal invitation we move into the second of the three great state rooms of this prayer, 'Your kingdom come.'

Here we are brought face to face with the glory of the Lord; he is the King of Kings. The whole universe is his; he is Lord over all beings, good and evil, heavenly and earthly. The very existence of earth's proud empires is in his hand and he laughs at the little human schemes that challenge his sovereignty. The whole earth is the Lord's, to him belongs all power and glory and majesty.

On a personal level, on entering this awesome room, we do well if we find ourselves holding our breath, walking on tip-toe, overwhelmed by the sheer magnificence of the One into whose presence we are bidden to come. Like the noble and godly prophet Isaiah of old, in the presence of the glory of the Lord, we find ourselves unworthy, undone and totally dependent upon his mercy.

In our own over-casual society, we need to be reminded of the awesome holiness and glory of God Almighty. The very nature of our heavenly Father, the one to whom we are invited to pray demands, not a cheery greeting but a bowed knee – and wonder.

The kingdom of God is variously described in the New Testament as, 'The kingdom of heaven,' 'The kingdom of God,' 'The kingdom of his beloved Son' and 'The kingdom of our Lord and of his Christ.' We are called to pray that this kingdom may come, but called to pray not in terms of armies and conquests, not, indeed, in terms of human rule or territory at all. For the kingdom of God is not of this world. It is a kingdom that leaps every kind of human boundary; it cannot be contained by prison bars or chains, it cannot be excluded by political or religious barriers. It is not at all like the passing and territorial kingdoms and empires of this world. It is, rather, like seed growing in each nation. In some societies it flourishes, in others it is crushed, in some it all but withers away. There have been seasons in British history when the kingdom of God has grown, thrived and been fruitful beyond measure. But in our own day widespread secular thinking, the pursuit of pleasure and the drive for material gain have all but choked it.

Where is the kingdom of heaven to be found?
Firstly, the kingdom comes here on earth where God the Father and his Son, the Lord Jesus, are honoured. As Jesus came to his own people, he said, 'The kingdom of God is among you.' He is the gateway, the door of the kingdom, he is the source of our forgiveness and wholeness. As people came and honoured him, so they became members of the kingdom. Zacchaeus, a hated tax collector for the occupying Roman overlords, was a man whose life was totally changed as he honoured the Lord; salvation came to his house. The kingdom came there.

Wherever God's kingdom or rule is found, there will be totally changed people; people who will live for God; people who know the Lord Jesus for who he is; people in whose lives God the Holy Spirit has taken up residence. The kingdom of heaven is the joyful acceptance of the rule of God within our own individual lives. It is a kingdom of grace and forgiveness, giving us a fresh new start as a disciple of Christ, as a child of God and as a citizen of the kingdom of heaven. The kingdom touches us one by one and, through our changed lives, touches our homes, the affairs of those around us and ultimately the affairs of cities and nations.

Then, secondly, the kingdom of heaven is found among disciples as they meet together locally. It may be in great congregations or in tiny groups in houses. Jesus said, 'Where two or three are met in my name, I will be there.' So, when we meet to pray together as brothers and sisters in Christ and to work together for the kingdom of heaven, Jesus promised that he, by his Holy Spirit, would be with us binding us together and giving a common mind. Groups of Christians gathered together to pray and encourage one another. Here is the kingdom.

Thirdly, the kingdom of heaven is among his people right across the world. From every nation, language and tribe, God is calling out a people for himself. Although our circumstances and cultures differ very greatly, it is thrilling, when we meet, to discover ourselves brothers and sisters in Christ, fellow citizens of his kingdom.

Finally, and supremely, the kingdom will come when the Lord Jesus returns. At present the Lord Jesus, his kingdom and his people can be sneered at, ignored and forgotten by the world at large. But that will not be so when he returns. To him has been given all authority. He will return, not this time in humility, but with great power and glory as King of Kings and as judge of all people. Then every knee will bow.

'Till he comes,' is a constant theme of the New Testament. We are to watch and pray; we are to be about our Father's business; we are to keep faith, we are to hold fast, 'till he comes.' That phrase can ring in our hearts and minds as a motivation for all we do and think.

Here, then, is the kingdom as it touches this world. It is where Jesus is honoured in individual lives, among his people both locally and internationally, and when he returns in glory.

In practice, how can we pray, 'Your kingdom come'?

The petition is very practical, for under this heading can come all our prayers concerning the shaping of our own lives; all our prayers for our loved ones and family; all our prayers for the people with whom we mix day by day at work, at leisure and in our local community. Only then, can we look out and catch the magnificent vision of our town, our country, our world won for the kingdom of God.

Every great house has its particular places from which can be seen the most magnificent views. Views not only over the formal gardens and estate but sweeping on over woodland, farmland and maybe out to sea. Such is the view given to us as we pray, 'Your kingdom come.'

The Great Commission to bring the gospel to the world is here in the phrase, 'Your kingdom come.' Here is the heart of all true mission and outreach. How then should we pray for missionaries of the gospel wherever they may be? What should be the content of our prayers?

– Pray, certainly, for their provision and safety and for God's overruling hand on their circumstances, all subjects of this great prayer, but supremely pray that our Father's kingdom may come:

– Pray that as they speak and seek to be alongside people, men and women, and young people may be touched by the Holy Spirit of God; that the Lord's presence and glory may be known amongst that people.

– Pray that as they train and encourage local Christians a local church may be born, the kingdom may come.

I shall never forget the impact of the words of a Kenyan pastor who, on coming to this country, was at pains to thank us as a people for sending out our finest sons and daughters to bring the gospel to Kenya the century before. How far would the bringing of the kingdom of God to an unknown and perhaps dangerous people feature in our hopes and ambitions for ourselves or for our children?

We need to pray that God's kingdom would come in our own land, too. We live in a land where, by and large, people have turned away from God, regard him as irrelevant. Pray, therefore, for spiritual revival; that we may turn again to him. Pray that God would revive his church and raise up those who will relevantly teach what the apostles taught. Pray that across our nation he will give people a spiritual hunger. The disciples were accused of filling Jerusalem with their teaching. May our cities and towns also be filled with faithful, godly teaching. Pray that men and women and young people might bow the knee to the Lord Jesus. Here is the grand purpose of fellowship groups, Sunday schools and youngsters' clubs – not just for friendship or entertainment but for the kingdom of God. Pray that, through them, God would raise up godly leaders in the church, godly leaders in politics, medicine, education and in every area of our national life. The purposes of God are tied up with the local church.

Do we share this longing that God's kingdom might come where we live; that the Lord God might touch lives, by his Holy Spirit, in and through our local church?

Finally, and least comfortably, as we pray, 'Your kingdom come,' we do well to pause and think about our own lives. 'Lord God show me where I stand before you, that I might not deceive myself, or wear a mask before others.'

In this great state room, if we have eyes to see the kingdom at all, we will find ourselves immediately unmasked and unworthy. We are challenged to examine ourselves to see if we, ourselves, are truly part of the kingdom; challenged, also, to see if the rule of God is touching every part of our lives.

We tend to put our lives in little packets, little compartments, all kept separately. The slot on Sunday morning or evening may well be 'very godly', but our heavenly Father wants us to be a people of integrity, all of a piece. Not just Sunday, but Saturday night and Monday morning; business, pleasure and worship all brought under his rule. It is too easy to think of whole areas of our life as being quite outside God's concern, areas that we couldn't possibly pray about or ask for the Holy Spirit's guiding or control. For example, anger, resentment, family relationships; or maybe, our use of time or handling of money; our sex life, ambitions or career. But should this be so? If we are truly disciples of Christ should we not be able to pray about each and every part of our lives and say, 'Lord, I want to please you, by your grace may your kingdom come, may your will be done, in this part of my life'?

In this simple petition our Lord inspires the question that every true disciple needs, constantly, to be asking: 'What would my Father have me to do for his kingdom? What part can I play? What gifts, what windows of opportunity has my heavenly Father given me to help build, strengthen or establish his kingdom locally, nationally, internationally?' Here, in so short a phrase, is the whole purpose of life! 'Your kingdom come.'

'Father, we thank you for your mercy towards us. In thankfulness may we honour you, not only with our lips, but in our lives. Hasten the day when your kingdom comes in every part of our own lives, in our homes, our churches, cities and throughout your lovely, but rebellious world, for the glory of your great and holy name.'

Questions for personal reflection or discussion

1. In our culture, have we lost the perspective of the awesomeness of God our heavenly Father? Are we more likely to approach him with a cheery greeting than with awe and wonder?
2. How has our heavenly Father chosen to re-establish his rule on earth? Could it be coloured on an atlas as an empire?
3. Can you think of someone you know whose life has been totally changed by becoming a member of the kingdom of heaven?
4. In what local group, known to you, can a foretaste of the kingdom of heaven be found?
5. In what way will the kingdom of heaven eventually touch every nation?
6. At present the kingdom of God can be ignored or sneered at – will it always be so?

In practice, how can we pray, 'Your kingdom come'?
1. Why should, 'Your kingdom come,' be most important in our praying for our friends and family?
2. How can such a simple petition be at the heart of all missionary and outreach work?

3. 'We cannot truly pray, "Your kingdom come," without it touching the way we live, our career, our prayer life, and the way we use our money.' Is this true? If it is, are we truly praying it?

4. How do we pray for our local church? What is the grand purpose of its services, groups and young people's work? Is it friendship and wholesome entertainment? Or is it the furthering of the kingdom of heaven?

5. How easy is it to packet parts of our own lives quite separately? Would we admit to having areas of our life that we have yet to bring under the rule of Christ?

6. Does Christian maturity lie in the direction of being disciples in every area of our lives, of being all of a piece, consistently Christian?

References

Isaiah before God – Isaiah 6:1-5
'Power and glory and majesty' – 1 Chronicles 29:11
'The kingdom of heaven' – Matthew 6:33
'The kingdom of our Lord and of his Christ' – Revelation 11:15
'The kingdom of his beloved Son' – Colossians 1:3
'Not of this world' – John 18:36
'The kingdom among you' – Luke 17:21
Jesus, the door of the kingdom – John 10:9
Zacchaeus – Luke 19:1-10
Nicodemus – John 3:1-8
'A new creation' – 2 Corinthians 5:17
'Two or three in my name' – Matthew 18:20
'From every nation, language and tribe' – Revelation 5:9
'Until he comes' – 1 Corinthians 11:26

'Watch and pray' – Mark 13:32-37
'In power and glory' – Mark 13:26 & 14:62
'Every knee shall bow' – Philippians 2:5-11
The Great Commission – Matthew 28:19&20

Your Will be Done

Godly living and dying

As we are led into the last of the three great rooms of this royal house of prayer, we find ourselves in an awesome and holy place, a place where we come face to face with both the ecstasy and the anguish of true godliness, a place where heaven touches earth: 'Your will be done on earth as it is in heaven.'

As if the rooms were linked by great double doors, this petition is all of a piece with the one before it, 'Your kingdom come.' It is found in the early texts of Matthew's gospel and some of those of Luke, and is an outworking of the same principle: that God's rule may be seen as we live in practical obedience to our heavenly Father's instructions and guidance.

How then shall we pray it? How should we apply it to the great sweep of human activity here on earth and also to our own particular circumstances and concerns? We can make this petition on many levels: personally, locally, nationally and internationally. It is a very spacious room and from its windows we can look out and pray for those we love, for our church, for our community, for our land and for our world. The great scenes of prayer are all here: 'Your will be done.'

It is a prayer with both an active and a passive side. Actively, we are called to pray for God's overruling hand on the affairs of this world, that his will may be done. Actively, we are challenged to pursue all that is in accordance with his will in our own lives and in the lives of those for whom we are responsible. Passively, we are called to accept what is his will, even when it is to our own personal discomfort or even anguish.

In heaven our Father's will is done gladly, willingly, completely and joyfully – may it be like that on earth. May there be a foretaste, a 'touch of heaven' about our lives, our decisions and our communities here and now under the pressures and in the cut and thrust of earthly living.

Firstly, personally and actively: 'Your will be done. May the way I live, all that I do and say be pleasing before you.'

The Lord is our pattern, he did as he taught. This petition is not just, 'Do what I teach.' He did it, lived it and fulfilled it: 'My meat and essential food, my first priority is to do the will of him who sent me.' What he said, he said as from the Father. What he did, he did to please his Father.

Here, then, is the all-embracing prayer for those who would follow the Lord Jesus, for those who really want to love God with all their heart, mind and strength.

It is a prayer for every stage of life. When we are young it is our parents who make the decisions. So parents might well pray, 'May your will be done as we bring up these little ones, teaching them love, discipline and right from wrong.' As we grow older we start thinking for ourselves about, for example, schools and particular subjects for study and so youngsters and parents begin to share the decisions.

'May your will be done; may your guiding hand be on our thinking.'

With growing independence, 'Your will be done,' will work itself out in prayers like these:

May my relationships with the world around me be honouring before you.'

'May I view its resources as a trust to be valued, used and handed-on, rather than to be selfishly exploited, polluted and destroyed.'

'May my treatment of animals be kind.'

'Show me the deep and hidden prejudices of my heart so that my treatment of my fellow human beings from different groups and cultures may be fair and just and pleasing before you.'

'May I constantly seek to use my days as you would wish me to.'

'May my work be done in a way that pleases you.'

'Your will be done, today – even Monday morning! – at work, at college, and at home.'

Work and money, love, sex, marriage, family life and leisure, attitudes to the world and people around us, they are all here! 'Your will be done.'

In the light of scripture, with its warnings, instructions, examples and commands, this petition, 'Your will be done,' enables us to examine ourselves. It is like one of the great wall mirrors so characteristic of stately homes. Here, as it were, is a mirror in which we can look at ourselves as God our heavenly Father sees us. As we look we are brought face to face with a reflection that challenges us and gives us an opportunity to put right each part of our lives before him.

'Father, may we learn your right way and live in a way that pleases you.'

Secondly, our Father's will for our lives accepted: *the passive aspect of this prayer.*

What a marvellous but terrifying pattern was set by the three Old Testament friends of Daniel. As a public test of loyalty to the state, we read that they were required to fall down and worship Nebuchadnezzar's great statue. Although they were the king's loyal subjects, in utter loyalty to the Lord God they were willing to face even death rather than offer such false worship. Their response to the king has much to teach us:

'Our God is able to deliver us from the furnace, and we believe that he will, but if not, let it be known to you that we will not serve your gods or worship the golden image.'

The three short words, 'But if not,' tell us that their stand was no mere fleeting act of rash bravado but a terrifyingly courageous submission to the will of God, to whom they had pledged their total loyalty. 'But if not,' words echoed by the Lord himself in the garden of Gethsemane as he faced the double agony of the cross. He knew full well that his Father was able to save him from that hour, yet he prayed, 'Nevertheless, your will be done.' As he looked ahead to the agony of the cross, our Lord taught his disciples to pray, 'Your will be done on earth as it is in heaven.' To do his Father's will was his constant aim and joy, as it can be for us, but in Gethsemane it was his agony, his passion.

Jesus knowingly set his face to go to Jerusalem. Events did not overtake him, he was not swept by overwhelming circumstances to his death. He came, as he had said, to do his Father's will. From the beginning he had accepted that this would mean his death. On several occasions he had taken the disciples aside to warn them of it, and yet humanly he shrank from it. 'Father, if this cup can pass,' –

the agony and the anguish of it – 'let it pass, but if not, may your will be done.' Our Lord accepted his Father's will, submitted to it, despite the suffering.

Locally, we have been called as a church to pray for a whole series of very sick people, called to pray that God in his mercy would restore them to health. In praying that his will be done we have needed to be ready to accept what comes from the hand of our loving heavenly Father, be it life and health or sickness and death.

Humanly, the Lord Jesus shrank from the cross. Humanly, we would hold on to those whom we love. How hard a lesson to learn: 'nevertheless, your will be done.'

John Calvin as he lay dying said: 'You are slaying me, Lord, yet it is enough for me to know that it is your hand that is slaying me.' Here is the way to pray, passively, 'Your will be done.' For even through sickness and in death we can bring honour to his name.

If we begin to pray it with understanding, we will find this great room of the Lord's Prayer, this petition, distinctly challenging and uncomfortable. It has within it a great reforming principle which, if really worked out rather than just repeated, will change our thinking, speaking and way of living. It will begin to make us Christ-like, holy.

'Heavenly Father, your will be done. May we not only hear the beautiful words of this prayer, but follow them, obey them, shape our living and our dying by them.'

Questions for personal reflection or discussion

1. What is meant by the active and the passive sides to this petition?
2. In what sense is the petition, 'Your will be done,' the all-embracing prayer for disciples?
3. In what ways does the petition touch our everyday living?
4. How hard is it to accept the will of our heavenly Father when it is not to our comfort or to the comfort of those we love?
5. How much is the petition, 'Your will be done,' reflected in our Lord's own life, ministry and death?
6. To what extent should this petition shape our own living and dying?

References

'My meat is to do the will . . .' – John 4:34
'Our God is able' – Daniel 3:16&17
'Nevertheless, your will be done' – Luke 22:39-42

Your Will be Done, continued

The great principle of godly government

As we look at this petition, we must begin and end with personal holiness of living. And yet, perhaps, like a guest in a great house, caught and challenged by our reflection in a large mirror we move rapidly out of its range to the comfort of a window where we can look out on the world. To view the world is far less personal and far less threatening!

Clearly, in heaven God's will is done willingly, gladly and joyfully. Cause it be like that throughout the earth. May our national and international policies, laws and treaties be godly. May they have about them a touch of heaven.

The apostle Paul urges us to pray widely and especially for kings and those in authority. When we hear that leaders of great nations are meeting to work out treaties, to hammer out understandings, or to work for a common approach to a rising evil – we are to pray. We are to pray that the Lord's will might be done; that the agreements might be just and based on honesty and integrity and that they might be pleasing before Almighty God.

Our heavenly Father is able to overrule the activities of quite unbelieving men and women. In the Old Testament we read of Cyrus, who cared nothing for God, and yet he was God's chosen instrument. It is not Washington, Beijing, Moscow nor any other human power centre that is in ultimate control. It is the Sovereign Lord who is in control. As Nebuchadnezzar had so painfully to learn, 'The Most High God rules in the affairs of mankind.' He is God; he reigns.

We are called to pray, 'Your will be done, knowingly or unknowingly, in international affairs.' So, read the newspapers, watch the TV and pray, 'Your will be done on earth.'

We live in a fallen world where, from time to time, men and women of fearful ambition will arise to crush and conquer those around them. We are only safe when the godly are most mighty. We are only safe when the greatest power is in the hands of godly people and godly nations. Only then can wild and destructive men be restrained. Only then can we live in safety, for, although they may make many mistakes, godly men and women can be trusted to use their power against an oppressor and trusted also not to use it for aggression.

Thank God for the peace we enjoy and pray for godly government and godly ways at every level of society. For on God, and on his good hand on all those entrusted with authority, depends the well-being of our nation and, indeed, of our world.

Archbishop Thomas Cranmer and his fellow compilers, with brilliant spiritual insight, taught us to pray for those in high government office just along these lines. He taught us to pray that they might faithfully and impartially administer justice for the restraining of all that is evil or corrupting and for the support and encouragement of all that is godly and excellent.

'That they may truly and indifferently minister justice to the punishment of wickedness and vice and to the maintenance of thy true religion and virtue.'

The old words sound hard in our day, and yet they carry the seed of all that it means to really pray, 'Your will be done,' throughout every level of society.

Modern thinking concerning government is that it should be morally neutral, not adjusting punishments and rewards to restrain evil and corruption and to promote good and godly ways, but simply to provide the necessary support to enable its citizens to enjoy a free choice of lifestyle, godly or ungodly, moral or corrupt. As a direct result of abandoning the biblical perspective of the God-given privilege and responsibility of government, well intentioned modern governments actually find themselves presiding over the moral collapse of society.

We need to recapture the biblical perspective so beautifully taught in these few words; words from the prayer for the church in the 1662 Book of Common Prayer – a prayer all but forgotten by the modern church.

It takes some unpacking because both the language and the times have changed. The little word 'truly' carries with it the biblical understanding that those set in any position of authority are answerable to God for their decisions and actions. We are not free agents in a position of power by chance, there to deliver our own opinions and do what we will. We are agents of God, put in that position of authority to look after the best interests of those for whom we are responsible.

Here is a prayer that those placed by God in any position of authority might discharge that responsibility faithfully before him.

When we use the word 'indifferent' we mean we do not care either way about some matter. But in Cranmer's day it meant even-handedness, showing no difference between rich and poor, strong and weak as justice is administered. It is a prayer for fairness and impartiality. And rightly so, for always the temptation is to be partial; to have one kind of justice for the prince and quite another for the pauper. The temptation is to caution the well-spoken driver of an expensive car and fine the leather-clad motor cyclist. There is great pressure to take note, as we are wined and dined, of the skilful presentation of the powerful business concern but overlook the simple letter of an ordinary person who is being crushed or abused by that concern in its pursuit of financial gain.

Here is a prayer that those appointed to administer justice might do so impartially before God.

'To the punishment of wickedness and vice.' That sounds harsh to our ears, and perhaps 'punishment' is too narrow. However, one purpose of government is to restrain evil; to associate some kind of high cost with wrong doing and so make evil more difficult to practise. This can certainly be done by fining or locking people up. But it can also be done by the passing of laws which so balance the rewards as to make it less desirable to practise life styles that would, directly or indirectly, wreck or undermine society. Here is a great principle of government: to restrain evil.

'And vice'? Vice is all that would corrupt and break down our society, all that would undermine godly living. The words 'vice' and 'corruption' have almost lost their meaning in our tolerant but ungodly society where all kinds of morality and immorality are accepted side by side.

In our pursuit of individual, adult freedom are we not increasingly in danger of failing to protect vulnerable groups? We have, for example, all but removed legal protection for the unborn child. We are in danger of repealing laws that would protect young people from sexual exploitation. And by allowing parenting partnerships to become so casual, we have exposed a great many young people to abuse either in the home or, as they flee from it, on the streets. Those in high places are called to restrain those who would exploit others and to protect the vulnerable.

'And to the maintenance of thy true religion and virtue' There is a negative, restraining role of government and there is also the positive encouraging, maintaining and supporting role, the helping forward of everything that is truly good and godly.

We are not called to pray that those in government would support church schemes and structures, or that they would take on themselves the church's great task. But we are called to pray that those who govern will pass laws that will enable and encourage the flourishing of true faith and godliness among the people. Sadly, in our own day we are increasingly seeing governments across the globe passing laws that hinder or suppress it.

The role of government is also to support and encourage all that is good and excellent, noble and true in society. It is to support and help forward the best, for example, of business practice, medical practice and educational practice as well as to support the best in social practice and family life.

There are godly members in our Parliament who realise that the traditional family, the key building block of any society, is under great pressure; is penalised rather than supported by our tax and benefit laws. They are concerned about it because it will undermine society, so they work and speak to put this right. Thank God for such men and women.

'Father, your will be done in terms of our national laws.'

But it comes closer to home than this, for most of us will find ourselves, at one time or another, in some position of authority where we must 'govern' in the broadest sense of this word. We govern as we play our part looking after a younger brother or sister, or as a parent, committee member, teacher, leader, shop-steward or manager. In each situation we are called to be faithful and impartial, to cast our vote and to do all in our power to restrain evil and promote good and godly ways.

So finally, to the root and source of the whole matter: 'Your will be done in our own lives.' We begin and end here because, frankly, this is the most difficult.

Here, within ourselves is the primary battle. Only by the grace of God and the work of the Holy Spirit in our lives can we begin to swim against the tide of human nature and live a life that pleases him, or even wish to do so.

Are we willing, faithfully and impartially before God, to play our part? Are we willing, publicly, to stand against all that is evil; all that would undermine or corrupt society, and to promote and support all that is godly, honourable and excellent? Are we willing, privately, for his holy ways to control our own living and speaking: at home, at leisure and in our business, social and political lives? Do we really want his will to be done on earth as it is in heaven?

The Lord's Prayer is perhaps not the charming prayer we thought it was! Whatever our position in society, it is an invitation to walk from time to time in very uncomfortable places!

'Father, grant us grace, wisdom and courage to stand for you. May "your will be done" not only by our passive acceptance of your will but also by our active standing against evil from within and without, and by our pursuing of all that would bring glory to your name and further the well-being of those around us.'

Questions for personal reflection or discussion

1. How important is it for disciples to read the newspapers or watch the news and pray, 'Your will be done'?
2. What lesson did Nebuchadnezzar have to learn?
3. 'We are only safe when the godly are most mighty.' What happens when evil people are most mighty: a) in the household, b) in the classroom, c) in the neighbourhood, d) in the courts of law, e) in the nation, f) in the world?
4. Do modern governments pass laws that steadily restrain evil and promote good?
5. Can you think of groups of vulnerable people who need to be protected by law?
6. If a government aims to maintain godliness, is there a distinction to be drawn between upholding 'religious institutions' and promoting true godliness of living?
7. Can rewards and penalties be rightly used to encourage good and godly ways?
8. There are many levels at which we can be given authority; called to 'govern' – from looking after a younger brother for half an hour, to being a world statesman. At what levels of 'government' are we personally involved? Can the principles set out in this study be applied to each level?
9. Our Lord said, 'For out of the heart come evil thoughts, murder, adultery, fornication, theft, false witness, slander.' It is not popular to think of restraining ourselves. However, do we need to recognise our personal weaknesses, and, by the grace of God, manage, govern or restrain, for example, pride, gossiping, dishonesty, cheating, lying, or a craving for wealth power or sex? Some of these come very naturally from the hearts of many of us.

10. If the things mentioned in question nine do not challenge us, what of seemingly small dishonesties, rudeness, letting others down. 'talking ourselves up' or occasional deceit?

References

'Pray for kings and those in authority' – 1 Timothy 2:1&2
'Cyrus, God's servant' – Isaiah 45:1-6
'The Most High God rules' – Daniel 4:24&25
'For out of the heart' – Matthew 15:19

As it is in Heaven

A shaft of sunlight

'Your will be done,' stern and glorious, yet through an open doorway we catch a glimpse of what is yet to be. Like a beautiful, sunlit conservatory or garden room, here is a glimpse of heaven. And beyond that heart-stirring glimpse is heaven itself, the whole garden; a place of incredible beauty and peace; a place where we can walk at ease with our heavenly Father. 'Today,' said our Lord to the penitent thief, 'you will be with me in Paradise.' Paradise is the garden of God.

The Lord teaches us to pray that our heavenly Father's will might be done here, on earth, as it is done in heaven. Here, we long to see God's name honoured and yet so often see it so trodden underfoot. Here we long to see God's kingdom come and yet see the fulfilment of our prayers so often frustrated or long delayed. We long to see eyes opened and hearts set on fire for God, and yet see them dulled and blinded by Satan or by preoccupation with wealth, pleasure and care. We long to see God's will done and yet find a clash of wills, our own as well as the determined will of godless folk around us. Here, we pray, live and battle that the glory of heaven might be seen. There, it is seen in all its fullness.

For our strengthening and encouragement our Lord turns our eyes and thoughts heavenward where his name is honoured, where his kingdom is complete and where his will is done perfectly, willingly and with joy. He teaches us to pray, 'Father, cause it to be like that on earth.' He gives us hope. He gives us a note of praise. He lifts our eyes, in the middle of the prayer, to catch the wonder of heaven. This heavenly note is there to stir, challenge and refresh us as we pray. It is a moment of praise, a shaft of sunlight, a turning of our eyes away from the struggles of earth to the glory of heaven.

We are very much rooted and grounded in this present world. It is very hard to think of heaven, and yet the Bible, throughout, is very 'heavenly minded'. It is constantly reminding us that our citizenship is not here, but in heaven.

Where then is heaven? When the first Soviet astronauts broke free from this earth's atmosphere, they took the opportunity to score a point for atheism by declaring from space that there was neither God nor heaven to be seen. And yet, they really only destroyed a false picture. God, who inhabits eternity, is outside of time and space. We have not broken out of time and space by breaking free of this earth's atmosphere. That is only a relatively small step. God is outside of the whole universe which is all part of time and space.

Another very basic question is: Who will be there? Matthew begins the prayer with the phrase, 'Our Father in heaven.' God, our heavenly Father, is there. He is there, says the apostle John, with the Lamb, who is the Lord Jesus; and around the throne are innumerable heavenly beings who do his will gladly, willingly and joyfully.

Destined to join them – and this is awesome, wonderful and almost beyond our comprehension – mere human beings like ourselves. This is our heavenly Father's great purpose on earth. He is calling out men, women and young people from every nation and tribe to be his own people here and now and ultimately to be with him, where he is, in heaven.

Who will be there? Sadly, there are those who will not be there. For where God is, in his very presence, there will be nothing ungodly, unholy, or impure. In the light of that, who can stand accepted before God? The very disturbing fact is that not one of us has a natural ticket for heaven. Our only hope is in God our heavenly Father who of his mercy has made it possible for us to be made acceptable before him. Here lies the heart of the Christian message. It is God's amnesty for fallen men and women. Forgiveness and an acceptability before God that is not our own – not earned by our good living or our good deeds, nor merited by our religious zeal – but freely given to those who humbly submit to the crucified and risen Son of God.

It is people who respond to our Father's mercy in the Lord Jesus who will be there in heaven. These are the people to whom he has given the right to be his sons and daughters.

The mark, the guarantee, of those who are citizens of heaven is the Holy Spirit of God at work in our lives; opening our eyes to see the kingdom of God, bringing us into that kingdom, enabling us to live for God and changing us little by little into Christ-like people.

In Charles Wesley's words:
Changed from glory into glory,
Till in heaven we take our place...

This process of being changed is the Holy Spirit's marvellous work in the life of a disciple. A changed life, an increasingly godly life, is evidence of the Holy Spirit's work and is the seal of our citizenship of heaven. Of course, the opposite is also true; religious interest or religious talk without changed habits of living, stand as a terrible warning sign.

We all want to be citizens of heaven. The other place, the alternative, is to be shut out from our Father's presence and is at all costs to be avoided. It is described in the Bible only in the most terrible terms of God's just anger and of suffering and loss, ruin and endless regret. It is described in terms of men and women, loved and made in the image of God, yet who have turned their back on God or lived in this world as if there were no God or as if they were not answerable to him. By doing so, we deny ourselves our true destiny and calling – to be the sons and daughters of our heavenly Father, citizens of heaven.

How do the apostles speak of heaven?

'I heard a voice from heaven,' writes St. John, 'saying to me, "Write this: From now on blessed, happy are those who die in the Lord."' Those who die 'in the Lord', who die in true faith, are happy, are blessed. And we will never feel the force of that word 'blessed' until we say 'how much to be envied' are those who die in the Lord. They are most to be envied because they are God's own people destined to be with him where he is.

As disciples we are children of earth, and yet our true citizenship is not here but in heaven. We pass our time here living for the Lord, but do so as pilgrims, we are passing through. It is for this reason that we must not bind ourselves too closely with the things of this world. We are here about our Father's business but our destiny is to be with our Father in heaven, to be with our Lord. The apostle Paul was torn as he wrote to the church at Philippi, he wanted to continue to encourage them and yet he longed also 'to be with Christ which is far better.'

Once we have grasped such a picture of heaven, we will see why 'to die in Christ' is of all things most to be envied. When we truly see it, it will directly affect the way we live here and now. It will affect our living and it will affect our dying. It will affect the way in which we come to view the dying of our loved ones. It is always terribly hard to let them go. When a loved one dies we are shattered, torn apart. God has set us in families and among friends with bonds of love and companionship that are so strong that in grief we are left absolutely desolate. And yet, if we have really taken hold of the fact that it is so enviable, such joy, to be with Christ; that it is a journey completed, a race run, that our loved ones in Christ have now reached home, then, surely, there is no greater comfort for those of us who are left. It is right to weep, our loss is terrible, but not for them, for they are at home with the Lord. They are safely in his hands. The Lord has taken them to be with him.

Such a grasp of heaven will also affect our approach to our own last day. Of course, we are built, as human beings, to hold on strongly; to live. And yet if we really have, as the apostle Paul had, an understanding of heaven, a real longing to be with Christ, an assurance of a welcome home by the mercy of God, then there will come a time when we know that there is no longer need to cling on to this life; a time when it becomes right to put ourselves in his hands to take us home. We can look forward to being with the Lord.

Visiting Tom, a man in a Manchester hospital, the conversation turned to heaven. Tom was dying and he knew it. He was only expected to live a few days. Suddenly, Tom was praying, putting into his heavenly Father's hands his own departure. It was very wonderful. Something of the glory and wonder of heaven shone through that prayer. It was unforgettable. Here was a man ready, prepared.

He knew that to be with Christ was far better and he longed to be there. He, too, was torn with loved ones at hand and yet he knew that his time had come and that to be with the Lord was what he really wanted.

Heaven – take hold of it strongly. To be with the Lord is far better. When it comes to the day of dying, those who die in the Lord are most to be envied.

The apostle John tells us that heaven is the place of freedom, freedom from oppression, freedom from suffering. We are mortal and we live in a fallen world where sickness and suffering form the backcloth of our human existence, particularly in our closing years. By God's grace the science of medicine can help us marvellously. Given grace to accept our situation, we can rise above suffering with great courage and patience. Sometimes, by the goodness of God, there is physical healing here and now. But ultimately the victory, complete freedom, is not found here but in heaven.

Again, in this life the world presses hard, sometimes very hard indeed. We have fellow disciples even now hounded, threatened, persecuted or shut up in prisons and labour camps under oppressive, atheistic or fanatically religious regimes. There are many occasions in both Old and New Testaments which speak of godly people and how, on occasion, the ungodly will hate them and deliberately delight in pouring scorn on their faith and crushing them mentally and physically. We may be scorned and ill treated here but in heaven the world can no longer cause us to suffer, we will be free, there will be no more tears.

Here on earth we are dogged with weaknesses and with great temptations. Paul, too, knew the weakness of the flesh. 'The things I long to do, I fail to do and the things I long not to do, I find myself doing.' That is the nature of this earthly life. But in heaven there is freedom, and freedom, also, from the limitations of this earthly body, from the limitations of time and space. Here there are things that we long to do, but because of our personal limitations or circumstances just cannot do. There, we will be able to do his will with perfect freedom.

Then in heaven there will be rest. The apostle John writes, 'They rest from their labours.' John was almost certainly for a time a slave labourer in the mines of the prison island of Patmos. He knew about the sweat and toil of this earth. John encourages us to think of heaven, not in sentimental terms of floating about on clouds playing harps (!), but as our Lord taught us to think about it in this prayer. It is a state of freedom from pressure, a state of creative rest and exhilarating activity, where God's will is done perfectly, gladly and joyfully. This is worship in the fullest sense. There will be singing, but not just singing. It will be singing coupled with service as we are freely about our Father's business. His will done, perfectly, in heaven.

Then there will be joy. 'In your presence,' says the Psalmist, 'there is fullness of joy.' We will be 'with the Lord', and with those whom we have loved and lost awhile. We will understand then with new insight all that has passed. Here we wrestle in a fallen world with many hurts and hardships. There, will be joy, fullness of joy, the joy of home.

Here, we run a race. Here, we fight a fight. There, in heaven, is laid up an inheritance, a reward, a joy, a homecoming, and most to be desired, the prize, the crowning words of the Lord Jesus Christ, 'Well done, good and faithful servant, enter into the joy of your Lord.'

So, in the battles of life sing from the heart, with John Newton,

> *Let the world deride or pity,* – For it will!
> *I will glory in thy name:*
> *. . . Solid joys and lasting treasure*
> *None but Zion's children know*

'Father, in our tears and battles, lift us, we pray, in hope and in praise to see the glory of heaven. Show us afresh that our citizenship, and the citizenship of all those on whom you have set your love, is not here but with yourself in heaven.'

Questions for personal reflection or discussion

1. Our heavenly Father's will done on earth in the way in which it is done in heaven. To what extent does that thrill and inspire you?
2. Does our culture, interest or position, lead us to naturally assume that we have a 'ticket for heaven'? Should we assume it?
3. What is the trustworthy seal or guarantee of our citizenship of heaven?
4. Does, the picture of the loss and ruin and endless regret of men and women having missed their true destiny, fill you with horror? Should it? Does it motivate you to action as it did so many of the great missionary pioneers?
5. 'God's own people are most to be envied.' Why?
6. How will firm a hold of the true Christian's citizenship of heaven affect our living, our dying and our reaction to the deaths of those we love?
7. 'Sickness and suffering form the backcloth of our human existence.' Hard though such a statement is, does it help us to

understand our world and our circumstances and help us to ask, 'Why not me?' rather than, 'Why me?'

8. Do we care as we should for those who suffer because they are disciples of Christ?

9. We know so little about heaven, but do the New Testament references to homecoming, rest, joy, freedom and 'well done' encourage and strengthen us to face the battles of earth?

References

Paradise – Luke 23:43
Citizenship in heaven – Philippians 3:20
The throne of God and of the Lamb – Revelation 22:3
'From every nation' – Revelation 5:9&10
'Blessed . . . are those who die in the Lord' – Revelation 14:13
'To be with Christ' – Philippians 1:22&23
Hated, 'for my name's sake' – Matthew 24:9, Matthew 5:10-12
   See also. Apocrypha, Wisdom of Solomon 2
'The things I long to do' – Romans 7:15
'They rest from their labours' – Revelation 14:13
'Fullness of joy' – Psalm 16:11
'With the Lord' – 1 Thessalonians 4:17 and Philippians 1:23
A race, a fight and a crown – 2 Timothy 4:7&8
'Enter into the joy of your Lord' – Matthew 25:21&23

Give us Today our Daily Bread

Strength and freedom to live

The honour of our heavenly Father's name, the coming of his kingdom and the doing of his will on earth as it is done in heaven. These form the three magnificent state rooms of this great house of prayer. They set the vision, goal and aim for the more practical petitions that follow.

The petitions for daily bread, a forgiving spirit and spiritual safety do not stand on their own any more than a cluster of kitchens, cloakrooms, store rooms and security rooms would be built in the place of a great house at the centre of a great estate! The kitchens and cloakrooms are only there to make possible the banquets and receptions of the great rooms, and so it is with this majestic prayer.

We are taught to pray for bread, not just for ourselves and our own comfort, but bread that we might be free from anxious care and so free to live for the glory of our heavenly Father. We are taught to pray for forgiveness and for a willingness to forgive, not to make us 'nice people', but to enable us to live for the Lord and to work together with one another as a team. And we are taught to pray for safety, again, not for our personal comfort, but rather that we might be able to live as free and faithful servants of the King.

For many of us, however, it is not until we arrive at 'daily bread' that we feel, "Ah, now the prayer really begins. Bread is something that really matters to me. Before it was 'spiritual' and hard to understand, but now we have arrived at 'bread' it really begins to be relevant." Fair enough, but this is only because it meets us where we are, rather than where we ought to be! Having missed the vision of the first three petitions, petitions that lie at the heart of the prayer, we are like the teacher's nightmare of youngsters on an outing to a great house, scurrying through the magnificent rooms with eyes only for the sweet shop!

Nevertheless, what an encouragement it is that God our heavenly Father cares about our stomachs! He cares about the things we need day by day; cares about these basic practical details. Samuel Johnson, who first gave us the dictionary, was once challenged about the amount of care he was taking over his stomach. Dr. Johnson replied, 'My dear sir, if I did not take good care of this place I would not be able to take good care of anything else.' It is a fair point, and this is precisely the reason why our Lord taught us to pray, 'Father, give us today our daily bread.'

Here in this petition are the kitchens, store-rooms and accounting rooms of the great house. They are there to keep the table supplied and to make possible the day to day running of the house. They are there to give freedom from anxiety by supplying all that is necessary, 'bread' for today and 'bread' for tomorrow; exactly the thoughts that lie behind this petition. The great difference to note is that our Lord is not talking about the grand and the luxurious but about the simple, basic necessities of life. Our Lord is speaking of physical provision; food to eat, of which bread is the basic example.

If God withholds our daily bread we will be so filled with anxiety that we will not be able to live seeking first the kingdom of heaven or living for God. We will be completely overwhelmed with anxiety. Our Lord was concerned that we should not be filled with such anxious care; that we should be able to live before him as his people free from this kind of pressure. Therefore, he taught us to pray, 'Give us today our daily bread.'

Bread is, of course, a picture and symbol of all that we need physically, mentally and spiritually to live in this world and in this human body in a way that brings honour to our heavenly Father.

Our physical needs

Primarily we do need food; food both for ourselves and for those who depend on us. At harvest time we acknowledge that:

'All good gifts around us

Are sent from heaven above '

Ultimately, all that we need comes by the good hand of God.

'Lord God, thank you for your provision of food, teach us to value those who farm, produce and distribute it and spare us from such poverty or famine that the things of God are forgotten because of our concern for bread.'

But 'daily bread' also includes all our basic human needs, for example shelter and warm clothing. We are taught in this petition to pray, 'Spare us from such poverty, war, civil unrest, lawlessness or family strife that we are forced out of our homes.' These things strike at the very roots of both godly living and of our physical well-being. Family breakdown and strife at home reduces too many in our society to isolated, rootless, homeless, bed and breakfast, bed-sit or cardboard-box dwellers with all the temptations and dangers of the street; exploitation, drugs and sexual abuse. War brutalises us and makes us of necessity killers of our fellow human beings, and in the extreme reduces us to hungry, threadbare refugees all but forced to steal and fight as we compete with one another for food and temporary shelter.

As the English Reformers spoke of 'daily bread' they said something rather surprising. They taught, 'When you pray for daily bread, pray first for the government.' Surprising but right, for on our government, their policies, and God's good hand on them, will depend whether we have wealth or poverty, enough or too little bread.

Pray that our government may be able to defend us from those who would bring us into subjection, for subject peoples are rarely free from poverty.

Pray, too, that they may be able to maintain justice within our society, for if our goods are constantly being stolen or if we are often defrauded then we shall very soon be anxious about daily bread.

Pray, also, for the fair distribution of wealth within society as this is very much a matter of government policy. Pray for our government, that they might have discernment, in the face of the many competing pressure groups, to have an open ear for those who speak for the truly needy and so fulfil their function before God, that each of us might have daily bread.

Pray for stable, godly government whose task it is to guard and oversee the just provision of our basic human needs. The reformers saw these things clearly and yet it is so up to date! Fresh and relevant after 400 years!

Our social and medical needs

Our basic human needs also include mental and physical health. We live in a fallen world where any of us may go through times when we are simply not able to manage; our job collapses, our home life collapses, our health or mental health collapses, our strength fails. Then we need to pray for courage, for practical and medical help, and personally, for godly strength to face each day and for a willingness, in such circumstances to let go our proud independence and be interdependent as God intended. For God, our heavenly Father, has given us one another, family, friends and the wider society, to provide for each other in our hour of need. In such an hour we are taught to pray for all that we need to face another day in a way that brings honour to our Father in heaven.

Our spiritual needs

Our Lord spent considerable time in prayer and meditation, he did not live by 'bread alone'. We, too, need spiritual nourishment if we are to live as God's people in this world. For example we need opportunity to be alone and quiet before God. We also need an opportunity to read and think about his word, spiritually feeding ourselves day by day. We need the help of godly speakers and writers who can explain God's word to us and help us to shape our thinking and our living to please him. We also need the fellowship, support and encouragement of Christian friends. These things are as basic and necessary as bread.

We live in a hard world where Christ is shunned and God is forgotten. Pray then for a godly graciousness and for courage. Pray for strength and wisdom to face particular, difficult situations. These things, too, are daily bread. We need them fresh day by day if we are going to live as God's people. Each day, pray: 'Fill me afresh with your Holy Spirit that I might live today in a way that pleases you.' These are prayers for 'daily bread' in the setting of the whole prayer – seeking first our heavenly Father's kingdom and his honour. Put them where they belong! These are not prayers for daily bread for our satisfaction, let alone for our personal comfort or pleasure, they are petitions that we might bring glory to God as we live in his world.

The part that is ours to play
Our heavenly Father's normal way of providing for our daily needs is by the skills he has given us to develop and use and by sweat and hard work. For this reason true prayer is dangerous! It always has a reforming, a life-style changing element in it. We have to be willing to be a part of the answer to our own prayer. We cannot truly pray for bread without being willing to work for it. We will only truly pray for better relationships with those around us when we are willing to guard our own tongues, change our own attitudes or control our own behaviour. We will only truly pray for spiritual nourishment and growth when we are willing to set aside time for our heavenly Father and his word and actually allow his word to shape our daily living. We are utterly dependent on God for all that we need; but, we have also a part to play by self discipline, by skill, clear thinking and by determined hard work.

Finally, a true commonwealth
Do notice, again, that as our Lord taught us to pray for daily bread he taught us to pray, 'Give us today our daily bread.' Not just me and my but us and our. We are part of a family, part of a society, part of a land and it is together we pray for bread. So, as God gives us bread, we are to remember our brother, our sister in need. He feeds *us* together, he gives *us* enough.

As the Reformers considered this they presented a great challenge. It was that those of us to whom God gives plenty are 'God's treasurers'. Our heavenly Father has placed us where we are, in order to help those in need. The Good Samaritan of the parable with his donkey, wine and money, 'chanced' to pass that way and find the man in trouble. He was equipped and able to help – and he did. As you pray, 'Give us today' and God graciously answers that prayer, don't forget; don't pass by your neighbour, your fellow disciple who needs your help.

'Why is it,' the visiting Western Christian was asked, 'that you Christians in the West have so much while we Christians in the developing countries have so little?' Great trading nations have always amassed wealth at the centre by exploiting those at a distance. We will not truly begin to pray for those with too little bread until it touches our own trading and purchasing practices, the brands we buy, our own pile of bread and our own bank balance.

'Give us today our daily bread.' what a marvellous and dangerous prayer! This is a prayer that challenges our natural complacency, selfishness and greed. If God is truly our Father he is the Father of those who have plenty and the Father of those who are in need. It is all too easy to piously pray, 'O God, feed the starving people of . . .' Real prayers of compassion will always be found to touch our wallet, purse, or bank account!

George Muller laid his orphanage table though he had nothing to set before his children. As he prayed, so the Lord stirred the hearts of those who had plenty to bring food for the orphanage. Our Father's economy always has two sides; sometimes it is our place to give, and to give generously, and sometimes to receive and to do so humbly and gratefully before God. There is to be a holy interdependence of love, compassion and justice between those who are truly sons and daughters of the living God.

True prayer is life changing. Our heavenly Father is calling out for himself a people who will truly be a commonwealth of individuals, societies and nations. Ungodly self-sufficiency, greed and selfishness will always militate against this, yet the vision of a true commonwealth lies here, right at the heart of the Lord's Prayer.

'Father, thank you for your provision of our daily bread. Thank you for the wealth that we have, personally and as a society. We thank you for human government and pray for your overruling hand on it. Help us to use all that you entrust to us in a way that pleases you and stir us to be fair and generous in our dealings with those who have too little.'

Questions for personal reflection or discussion

1. How do you react to the suggestion that we pray these petitions for daily bread, forgiveness and safety, not for our comfort but so that we are free to live for God; free to be about our Fathers business?

2. Why do we need to pray for our government as we pray for daily bread?

3. Both nationally and individually we like to think of ourselves as strong and independent 'towers of strength'. But are we? Should we be? Can we be, when in the tough situations of life?

4. Do our prayers have a reforming, lifestyle-changing element about them? Are we willing, at our own expense or effort, to be our heavenly Father's answer to our own prayers?

5. How can the petition for daily bread touch and enlighten the selection of the goods we buy?

6). 'Real prayers of compassion will almost always be found to touch our time and money; our wallet, purse, bank balance and, maybe, our career.' How easy is this? Is it true? Does it happen?

7). The vision of a true commonwealth is right here in the Lord's Prayer, what stops it happening?

References

Free from anxious care – Matthew 6:25-33
'Bread alone' – Matthew 4:3&4
'Not work, not eat' – 2 Thessalonians 3:10-12
Good Samaritan – Luke 10:33-35

Forgive us our Trespasses

A fresh clean start

A humble, though essential, room in any great house is the boot room, a room full of pegs and racks, hats and coats, boots and shoes of every kind and size. Although the great doors will be opened and the carpet rolled out on occasion, this humble boot room is the essential way in for family members.

Near-by will be found a wash room. It may be outside in the courtyard or in the house very near the boot room. Together these practical rooms make it possible for household members to be made acceptable in the house. For you enter the house not across velvet lawns, but across real lawns with worm casts and mud. You enter from the mess of the stables or the mud of the estate and these humble rooms are the way in. Here you wash and leave behind your soiled boots and your outer clothing, garb totally unacceptable within the house. It is simply not acceptable to sit at table, on a beautifully embroidered seat, unwashed, in dirty boots and muddy over-trousers!

Our heavenly Father, too, has made provision for those soiled by the real world in which we live; provision for us to be made acceptable. The rooms are rooms of mercy, cleansing and forgiveness, and all true members of the household must pass this way and do so often.

'Forgive us our trespasses as we forgive those who trespass against us.' – The forgiveness of little things and the forgiveness of very great things; our Father's forgiveness of us and our forgiveness of others.

We look first at the beginning of the petition; God's forgiveness of us, 'Forgive us our sins, our trespasses, our wrong doing.' Such a prayer is basic to our spiritual well-being and standing before God. We must first come into our heavenly Father's presence, as our Lord has taught us, and simply pray, 'Forgive us our trespasses, our sins.' What does that actually mean? 'Set us free from our total debt', is closer to the Greek. But, even so, what is our debt to God our heavenly Father? What debt do we owe to the One in whose hand is our very breath and to whom we owe our very existence?

We owe him love. He brought us into being for his pleasure, to give him glory in our lives and to enjoy him forever. We owe him a debt of love, practically expressed in doing what pleases him.

We owe him a willingness to refrain from all that would pollute us before him; to steer clear of all that we know to be active disobedience or rebellion against him. However, by nature we tend to ignore what God requires, doing what we want and failing to do his will.

Our heavenly Father has commanded us to love him with all our heart, with all our mind, and with all our strength, to put him first. But who among us has truly so loved him? Religious words may slip easily from our lips, but what of the basic self-centredness of our day by day living?

When King David prayed his great prayer of confession, which we find in Psalm 32, he did not say, 'Blessed is the man who has not sinned, who has no need of forgiveness,' but rather, 'Blessed is the one whose sin is forgiven, whose debt is paid.'

Where, then, does forgiveness, the clearing of our debt begin? Paul the apostle speaks of the disciples at Corinth as having been taken from a very grubby world, washed and set apart for God by the cross of our Lord. The apostle's list of the goings-on in that port city of Corinth is as ancient as it is modern. Greed, theft, drunkenness, violence, perversion and vice are all there. The church at Corinth was composed of men and women taken from such a background and yet now, wonderfully, forgiven, adopted and made members of God's holy family.

The apostle Paul uses the picture of washing as he describes how they were made clean, made acceptable before our heavenly Father. So here, in the great house, are these very practical rooms, wash rooms and bathrooms. We may need to begin first in an outside wash-house, for some of us are as well soiled as a dog that has rolled and besmirched itself in some canine delight that brings no delight to its owner and indeed makes it totally unacceptable in the house. 'A stench or stink in the nostrils of God,' is exactly how sin and godless ways are described in the Old Testament.

We may never have so deliberately soiled ourselves, and yet no matter how privileged, how well brought-up, how respectable we may be, when our eyes are opened, each one of us will find ourselves soiled and unacceptable before God.

Isaiah, the Old Testament prophet, was both noble and godly and yet, when face to face with the glory and holiness of the Lord, he found himself totally unacceptable, ruined and undone. The memorial stone of a godly and respected local Squire from Victorian times simply begins with the verse: 'God be merciful to me a sinner.' Words that reflect his own plea before God and leave a signpost and an encouragement for those who read them today.

Why do we need forgiveness? What makes even the most privileged and refined of us totally unacceptable before God? Why are all our best efforts and fairest offerings only like 'filthy rags'?

Our need of forgiveness is hard for us to see for a number of reasons. For one, if we are not guilty of specific acts like murder, theft or adultery we assume we must be fine. Then again, we are so ready and eager to forgive ourselves that we cover over or make a very small matter of any 'slight indiscretion' before God. Why, it was hardly worth noticing and we can always provide a thousand reasons why we really could not help it or why it was not our fault! The fact is that we stand accused by precisely these deep-seated, self-centred habits of mind and body to which we are, by nature, totally blind.

At rock bottom, we need forgiveness because by nature we live in God's world as if there were no God. – Perhaps not in the great crises of life or when we desperately need something – but by and large we ignore the God in whose hand is our breath. In the words of the Lord's Prayer, we fail to honour him, fail to seek first his kingdom and right ways, fail to do his will, much preferring to do our own will. We also fail to love those around us in the way in which we love ourselves. These are the self-centred, God-ignoring ways that the Bible calls sin, a stink, and that cause us to be totally unacceptable before Almighty God, the righteous judge, and so in desperate need of mercy and forgiveness.

The true sons and daughters of God are like street children taken from the filth, violence and vice of the city and adopted into a royal household. The first step is a complete wash and change of clothes. Here is mercy; here is the forgiveness of God, here we are given a fresh new start. Thereafter begins the very gradual, faltering process of a total change in the basis of our thinking and acting. We slowly learn to love the Lord who made us acceptable and adopted us into his family. We begin to long to please him; to put the Lord God, rather than ourselves, at the centre.

God our heavenly Father has made it wonderfully possible for each one of us to be made acceptable before him. No matter how soiled, we, too, may be made sons and daughters of the living God, not on the basis of our own goodness or merit or worth but by the mercy and forgiveness of God, found in our Lord Jesus Christ, who came to this world for our rescue; came to lay down his life for us, for our forgiveness. On this basis our Father is most willing to forgive. He is more willing to forgive than we are willing either to admit our need of forgiveness or to humbly ask for it.

This is the great and primary application of these words. We will often need to return to confess and wash away the grime of real, everyday living in this world as a child of God, but never again for the radical treatment that first brings us into the household.

'Heavenly Father, forgive us our trespasses, have mercy on us, write off our debts once and for all, put us right with yourself. May we, like the ancient Corinthian Christians, be washed and made acceptable before you.'

Questions for personal reflection or discussion

1. How natural is it to excuse, cover over or make a very small matter of our own failures before our heavenly Father?
2. 'Failed to honour him, failed to seek first his kingdom, failed to do his will' – to what extent is the Lord's Prayer itself a mirror in which we can see our own falling short and so see our own need of forgiveness?

3. Where do we stand, personally, if even the noble and godly Isaiah found himself totally unacceptable before the holiness of the Lord?

4. 'A fresh new start – like street children taken, washed and adopted into the family.' How well does this describe the beginnings of discipleship?

5. 'The very gradual, faltering process of a total change in the basis of our thinking and acting. We slowly learn to love the Lord.' How well does that describe our own spiritual pilgrimage or walk with our heavenly Father?

6. The apostle Paul expressed what it is to be a forgiven child of God in words like these: 'living by faith in the Son of God who loved me and gave himself for me,' and 'the love of God shed abroad, flooding our hearts by the Holy Spirit who has been given us.' Could we echo such expressions?

Footnote, a personal prayer for forgiveness

'God have mercy on me a sinner.'

Almighty God and heavenly Father, I acknowledge that I have not honoured you as I could and should have done. I have failed to play my proper part in the building of your kingdom. By my unwillingness to do what you have asked us to do, and by my persistent doing of those things you have asked us not to do, I have been failing to do your will.

Have mercy on me, forgive me and give me a fresh new start. I ask this in the name of your Son, the Lord Jesus Christ, who, the Scriptures plainly teach, laid down his life in order that we might be spared from your just judgment and freely forgiven. Stir me, prompt me and fill my life with your Holy Spirit so that I might truly repent, turn from ungodly ways and live to bring honour to your holy name. Amen

References

'To love him with all our heart' – e.g. Mark 12:28-31
Corinthians 'washed' – 1 Corinthians 6:9-11
A stench, sin abhorrent – Genesis 6:5-6
Isaiah unacceptable before God – Isaiah 6:1—5
'God be merciful' – Luke 18:13
'Filthy rags' – Isaiah 64:6
Open confession before God – 1 John 1:5-10
'Came into this world for our rescue' – 1 Timothy 1:15
'Living by faith in the Son of God' – Galatians 2:20
The love of God poured into our hearts – Romans 5:5

Forgive us our Trespasses, continued

Ongoing, day by day forgiveness

Having been made a child of God by his mercy, we will often need to return to confess and wash away the grime of real, everyday living in this world but never again to make that initial cry for forgiveness, 'Lord, have mercy on me', that first brings us into the household.

As adopted members of our Father's family, we shall want to leave each day's mud behind as we enter the house. Both the boot room and the washroom are rooms of repentance and confession, rooms of cleansing and forgiveness. They give us a moment to reflect on the day: 'Father, these are the opportunities that I missed to serve you, to honour you, to speak for you, to love my neighbour. These are the things I have failed to do. These are the things that I did in haste, anger, or in foolishness, at home, at work, in society.' Scripture urges us not to hide or cover them over, not to belittle them as being of very minor importance, but to come openly to our heavenly Father. Such prayers are no longer in terms of our acceptability before him, our place in the family, but rather in terms of our walking with our heavenly Father at ease and in the joy of a right relationship.

If we pray it aright, the wonder of the Lord's Prayer – and, indeed, the wonder of all true Christian living – is that it will change us, it will reform the way in which we live and so we will grow as disciples.

Sadly, there is a lot of religious activity which does not change us at all. We go and do certain things in a compartment of our lives we call 'worship'; it may be with colour and candles and beautiful, traditional music, or it may be with stirring, modern music, shining faces and uplifted arms. We enjoy it. It moves us at the time. But it does not change us; it does not touch the rest of our lives. We go on living exactly as we had done before.

However, if we really pray the Lord's Prayer from the heart it will change us. We will find that as we bring our trespasses day by day before our heavenly Father, our conscience will be awakened and sharpened. We will be more aware of our Father giving us opportunities to serve him and also, increasingly, painfully aware of the opportunities we miss. We will begin to be aware of those things that do not bring honour to his name, even before we do them. We will begin to long not to do them. By the grace of God and the prompting of his Holy Spirit, we will be changed. This gradual changing is the purpose of God for each one of us; that we might be more Christ-like. Hence this prayer, 'Forgive us our sins, our trespasses, our debts,' will need to be often on our lips if we are to grow as disciples.

Our communal failings

Like all these petitions, the prayer for forgiveness is set in the Lord's Prayer in the plural; not 'me' and 'my' but 'us' and 'our' sins, debts and trespasses. Although our heavenly Father chooses to deal with us one by one, giving us an individual walk with himself, we are set in communities. Like a stone thrown into a pond, we begin with personal confession, but the ripples move out to affect the whole surface. As we really begin to pray we will look beyond our own personal standing and walk before God. We will begin to see and acknowledge our collective responsibilities and failings before our heavenly Father.

Throughout the Old Testament of the Bible, there are many examples of godly leaders crying to God for forgiveness, not only of their own failings, but of the failings of those around them.

For example, we read of:

Moses pleading with the Lord not to destroy the people of Israel who had so soon turned their back on God and were worshipping an idol; a calf they had made from gold.

King Josiah, humbling himself and seeking the Lord when he discovered that his people had not been keeping God's law.

Job rising early in the morning to confess the possible sins and excesses of his sons as they feasted and celebrated in one another's houses.

Nehemiah, that man of God who so strongly held together prayer and action, hearing of the trouble and shame of his fellow countrymen who had escaped the exile, sat down and wept and fasted, pouring out the failings of his people before the Lord God. See him pleading with the Lord to hear the prayers of those who fear him and grant mercy and success. Secretly he wept and prayed and cried for forgiveness, publicly he asked the King's permission and went and rebuilt Jerusalem's walls.

Daniel, confessing his own and his people's failure, pleading with the Lord for mercy, and that for the honour of his name, he would restore his ancient people and their city.

Here in Britain, we live in a land that has been the centre of an empire. Do we need to look afresh at our national pride and arrogance, and at our collective 'blind eye' to the commercial exploitation of those who produce the food and goods we buy so cheaply?

We are part of a society that is still greedy and generally unconcerned about our use and our abuse of the environment.

We live in a land that has been so blessed of God. He has had such patience with us and spared us so many times and yet, as a people, we are turning away from him, ignoring him at every level. We cling to our ungodly and materialistic lifestyle and ignore the God in whose hand is our very existence. 'Father, forgive our wilful forgetfulness of your goodness and turn us again, as a people, to godly ways.'

God has given the historic churches of our land very great privileges and very great spiritual responsibilities. By and large, we have enjoyed the privileges but have failed in our great responsibility to uphold godly ways in our land and to win the people of each generation for the Lord. 'Father, forgive the coldness, the formality and the absorbing self-interest of our churches, and kindle afresh courage, love and vision.'

Finally, and so significantly, we live in a society in which so many people now place the bringing up of children, and particularly their spiritual welfare, well down the list of priorities, well below the pursuit of their own career or of their own personal happiness. But before God the family has a far greater priority, for godly society depends on godly parents.

Our families really are the basic building blocks of community living and of a godly society. They are the seedbed of love, trust and stability. They are given to be the royal nursery for the rising generation. They can also be the guest rooms for godly hospitality. Our homes are the setting where godly love can be shown to our neighbour and where justice, compassion, forgiveness and faithfulness can be learned and practised by parents and children together.

In our pursuit of wealth and personal happiness, we so easily forget that our heavenly Father's priority is the raising of godly offspring. The debt we owe is to use our homes for the Lord; especially to do all in our power to faithfully bring up the youngsters he has entrusted to us to know and honour the Lord. 'Father, forgive us.'

As a land, as a church, as a society and as individuals we have fallen so far short.

'Father, have mercy. Forgive us our neglect, our failure, our wilful blindness and disobedience – our trespasses, and give us a hunger to live to please you.'

Questions for personal reflection or discussion

1. What distinction is drawn between our first becoming disciples and our day by day need of forgiveness as members of the family?
2. 'Father these are the things . . .' In what ways can admitting our need of forgiveness each day enable us to grow as disciples?
3. 'Oh, that singing was so uplifting!' or, 'I could listen to that preacher for hours.' What hidden danger could lie behind such appreciative words? (See the first paragraph of the second page of this chapter.)
4. In what particular ways is our church and our whole society in need of repentance, a turning away from wrong thinking and doing, and of the forgiveness of our heavenly Father?
5. Of what 'blind spots' could we be guilty?

6. In generations to come, will our exploitation and pollution of the planet be as unthinkably dreadful as the slave trade of the 1700s is to our eyes now?

7. We find ourselves entrusted with the care of God's beautiful, yet spoiled and hurting world. As individuals and as a nation, are we honouring him in the way we are looking after it?

8. To what extent are our homes 'the royal nurseries of the rising generation'? What are our priorities in home life? Are they as God-centred as they should be?

9. The caption under a picture of a father earnestly praying for his sleeping, young son simply reads, 'Spiritual Warfare'. Do we know anything of such warfare? Have others engaged in it for us?

References

'Lord, have mercy on me' – Luke 18:13

Open confession before God – 1 John 1:5-10

Moses – Exodus 32: – 13

Josiah – 2 Kings 22:11–20

Job – Job 1:4&5

Nehemiah – Nehemiah 1:4-11

Daniel – Daniel 9:1-19

Godly offspring and family priorities – Malachi 2:14-16

Bringing up youngsters – Ephesians 6:1-4

As we Forgive those who Trespass against us

Eager and ready to forgive

We have looked first at the forgiveness that God offers us, as this is absolutely basic to our standing before him. We all stand before God as sinners or 'debtors' in need of mercy. We come, as it were, with empty and soiled hands and with nothing to offer except the prayer, 'Forgive us our trespasses.' In his mercy, our heavenly Father is willing and able to clear our debts, make us acceptable before him, citizens of his kingdom and his adopted sons and daughters. Here is the goodness of God. Here is forgiveness and mercy. Great and wonderful it is; more precious, says our Lord, than the finest of pearls or the greatest of treasures.

We look now at the second part, 'As we forgive those who trespass against us.' At first sight it seems as if the Lord could be teaching that we can earn or deserve God's forgiveness if we forgive others. But can it mean that? Could we ever earn forgiveness before God? Before him, even our best efforts are contaminated; our fairest offerings are only, as Isaiah so vividly describes them, 'filthy rags'. We have fallen so far short that we are never humanly able to put things right. Reconciliation is all of God's goodness. To teach that we can earn God's forgiveness is to go against the whole teaching of our Lord and the whole of the Apostles' consistent teaching.

Rather, the Lord is reminding us that as we have known and tasted the wonderful mercy and forgiveness of God, so we must reflect it in our day by day dealings with those around us. Having been forgiven we must be eager to forgive those who have wronged us. We must not be like the unmerciful servant of the Lord's story who owed his master a vastly great amount. Being totally unable to pay, he was freely and graciously forgiven, but he then went out and showed no mercy whatever on his fellow servant. The unmerciful servant was freely forgiven by his master – but by his behaviour to his fellow servant he lost, he forfeited that forgiveness. We can never earn God's forgiveness. But here we are solemnly warned that we can forfeit forgiveness. Our heavenly Father will not continue to have mercy on us if we ourselves remain stubbornly unforgiving.

Our Lord is teaching us to pray: 'Father, as you forgave me, give me a forgiving spirit. As you have been merciful and generous to me, may I be merciful and generous to those around me.'

Such a willingness to forgive is the exact opposite of our basic human nature. By nature, we demand from others 'justice', our 'rights', our 'pound of flesh', but for ourselves beg to be excused and shown mercy.

Again, the godly forgiveness we are shown here will never be either easy or tidy. We will be forced on each occasion to find the right balance between the harshness of justice without mercy and the softness of mercy without justice. We are to be generous and merciful – yet not to so abandon justice that people mock us and take advantage of us. Our heavenly Father well understands this, for in the cross of our Lord Jesus both justice and mercy play a full part, justice is satisfied as mercy is freely offered. We are to forgive as we have been forgiven.

In this second part of the petition we move from the wash room and boot room, where we are made acceptable, to the chapel. Here, in this quiet and lovely room, built and furnished to enable prayer to be as natural and easy as breathing, we can quietly reflect on our Father's patience and mercy towards us as we wandered and strayed or as we wilfully ignored him. Here, together or alone, we can draw strength and resolve to honour our heavenly Father in our dealings with those around us. We can resolve to be forgiving as we have been forgiven.

What does it mean 'to forgive'? The word itself means 'to send away' or 'to put away'. Forgiveness is the putting away of the things that would keep us apart. The aim of forgiveness is that two persons or parties estranged by a wrong or trespass might be reconciled and brought together. To bring this about, the wrong needs to be put away. God is willing to put away our debt before him. We must be willing to put away the offences and trespasses that are committed against us; to put away, on our part, anything that would stand in the way of reconciliation.

The quiet resolve before God to be forgiving needs to be carried into the cut and thrust of daily living and so we must move from the beauty and quietness of a chapel – where to be spiritually minded is easy – to the home, the work place and the neighbourhood where it most certainly is not.

Forgiveness of ourselves
The forgiveness of this second part of the petition is primarily about our relationship with others – and yet we do need to learn to forgive ourselves as God has forgiven us. The evil one, the accuser as he is sometimes called in scripture, will constantly play on and remind us of our past failings, our guilt, our secret sins and weak-

nesses or our ineffectiveness. However true the accusations may be, once they have been brought openly before our heavenly Father and his forgiveness sought, then every time we are reminded of them and tempted to be cast down by the memory of them, our strong response must be, 'Yes, sadly true, but my heavenly Father knows about these things, the debt is paid, and all he requires is that I live today for him as his forgiven child.' If God has 'put away' our wrong doings and our failures so must we, so that we are set free to live in the present for him.

Forgiveness of those we know well
The moment we become really close to someone in friendship, courtship, marriage or as a colleague at work or leisure we discover that they are not quite perfect! It is a well established phenomenon that when a new clergyman or minister comes to a church, for the first months he is thought wonderful, fresh and bright and clearly the answer to all the church's problems, and can do nothing wrong. After a couple of years he cannot do anything right and after a couple more they know his every odd mannerism and expression so well that he is merely tolerated or ignored. You can see the wisdom of moving often! More seriously, it is a good illustration of the fact that when you really get to know someone you find that they are not the perfect person you imagined them to be but a frail human being with failings and weaknesses, blind spots and annoying habits; in fact, a human being in need of help and constant forgiveness.

Young people setting up home soon discover the same thing. Indeed, the first year of marriage is notoriously difficult. The lady finds that her 'prince charming', though wonderful in the days of courtship, loses his charm as he sits sullen and unshaven over unpaid bills and cornflakes!

We need to learn forgiveness towards those closest to us. They will let us down. Our personal, treasured little ways may be upset or our possessions spoiled. We need a constant spirit of forgiveness in order to take in our stride the many annoyances. Talk them out, sort them out, but do not gather them and nurse them as growing, unforgiven resentments.

Godly leaders of a former generation referred to family life as 'the boiling pot, the cauldron of our sanctification'; the place where true holiness of living both grows and is tested to the limit! In our homes, a willingness to ask for forgiveness, and to freely give it when it is asked of us, lies at the heart of our growth as disciples of Christ.

'Lord, as I have been forgiven, give me a forgiving spirit; kindness to those around me'

Forgiveness in our society

In our neighbourhood or workplace our property may be damaged by a careless colleague, a neighbour may deliberately or unwittingly upset us, or we may be the subjects of false rumours in local gossip. The Lord is teaching us in these difficult situations to be willing to forgive; to grow, as a fruit of the Holy Spirit, a willingness to be patient; an eagerness to sort out misunderstandings in a straightforward way and to seek reconciliation.

Forgiveness of terrible wrongs

In this fallen world we can be really hurt, really let down, seriously offended against and owed much. What should we do then? What should our attitude be? In the New Testament, it comes across very clearly that there are conditions to forgiveness. The father of the prodigal son in our Lord's parable was desperately let down and yet ran to meet his son. He was ready and eager to forgive and to be reconciled with his reckless son.

However, there could be no forgiveness, no reconciliation, until that son 'came to himself' and became willing to admit his mistakes and return home. Such a willingness to face the truth and offer an apology is never easy. 'I'm sorry, I was wrong', are perhaps some of the hardest words to say. It took a famine and the pigs' trough to bring the son to that point! But there must be this turning, this repentance, if there is to be any true forgiveness or reconciliation.

Having said that, if those who have terribly wronged and hurt us seek our forgiveness and an opportunity to put things right, we must be as willing and as eager to forgive as the father of the prodigal son who rushed to welcome and reinstate the filthy but returning lad.

Moving into a yet larger scene, as God's children wanting to honour him by reflecting his mercy, what of those who deliberately hurt and maim and destroy; who deliberately steal and cheat? What of those who would scoff at your willingness to forgive and who have no intention of seeking reconciliation?

We sometimes hear people say, 'I could never forgive, she cheated me of my husband, he cheated me of my wife, he abused my child, they killed my son. I can never, never forgive.' But supposing it was our son or our daughter, could we, should we ever forgive? Human nature cries out that those who hurt and maim and kill should never be forgiven, but how should the disciple, the forgiven child of God react?

At a Remembrance Service in Northern Ireland a bomb was detonated and a Christian man lost his much loved daughter. That father was able to bear no malice, no hatred, towards those who killed her. That is the Christian reaction. You cannot forgive where there is no desire for reconciliation, but you can offer it, you can be willing to forgive, you can bear no malice. From the cross, our Lord Jesus himself prayed, 'Father forgive them.' He did not declare them forgiven. He prayed that they might come to the place where they might be forgiven, and there find forgiveness freely offered.

Agents, together, of justice and peace
'To bear no malice,' as that applies in each of our own personal lives, it also applies to groups of people. There can be great feuds between families, tribes and nations; people determined never to forgive or be reconciled and living with resentment, hatred and bitterness. People living with a determination to be avenged stored up as part of their community heritage and identity. Here is the basis of the great divides, hatred, hostility and, too often, war.

What part can disciples play in such situations? Our Father's economy is always based on his people being peacemakers; praying, working and seeking for reconciliation; being willing to forgive. And so it becomes plain that forgiveness is a matter both for individual disciples and for disciples together. Hence the 'us' and 'our' and 'we' of the Lord's Prayer – 'as we forgive'.

At school my German teacher, under Hitler's regime, had lost everything – his home, parents, brothers and sisters: everything. He escaped to this country and twenty years later he was teaching German. But he was doing more than that. He was a godly man, and he used his position to arrange exchange groups with German families. This man had been hurt so deeply and yet here he was working for reconciliation. By the grace of God he was free from bitterness. Having personally forgiven, he was able to be a peacemaker.

Here is peace-making, forgiveness in practice. It is personally very costly but there is about it – a touch of heaven.

Humanly it would be easy to justify an attitude of contempt, hatred or revenge. But, by the grace of God, may our lives be free from these things and marked by an openness to reason, a bearing of no malice, an eagerness for reconciliation – a willingness to forgive as we have been forgiven.

This prayer for a forgiving spirit is like another great wall mirror in which we can see ourselves. It is an immediate test of our own calling and standing before God as it accurately reflects our relationship with our heavenly Father. Have we truly tasted the mercy of God? Do we long to reflect that mercy in our dealings with those around us, both in the little things and in the great hurts of life? Do we really want to see his name honoured and his kingdom come – even in the matter of forgiveness?

'Lord God, have mercy on us. Help us to recognise our own natural and inbuilt lack of mercy. Give us a forgiving spirit. Give us grace individually and together to put away bitterness and hatred and to forgive those who trespass against us, as we have been forgiven, that your holy name may be honoured and your will done.

Questions for personal reflection or discussion

1. To what extent is it human nature to be like the unmerciful servant, taking forgiveness offered to us for granted but being none too hasty to forgive those around us?

2. Why should we be willing and eager to forgive?

3. How easy is it to love justice and show mercy?

4. Is it sometimes almost hardest of all to forgive ourselves? Yet, can we, should we, must we? Why?

5. 'Not perfect, but with weaknesses, 'blind spots' and annoying habits – a human being in need of help and constant forgiveness.' How well does that describe those close to us? How well does it describe us?

6. 'I'm sorry, I was wrong.' When these words are really meant, are they some of the hardest words to say? Why?

7. Can there be true reconciliation without a willingness to admit our mistakes?

Forgiveness of terrible wrongs

1. In what situations do we need to, 'bear no malice'? Are we willing to be searching for and eager to welcome the first hint of a move towards reconciliation?

2. Have you known or read about people whose Christ-like willingness to forgive has challenged you?

3. In what ways and in what situations would our heavenly Father have us be peacemakers?

References

'Pearls' or 'treasure' – Matthew 13:44&45

'Filthy rags' – Isaiah 64:6

The unmerciful servant – Matthew 18:23-35

Stubbornly unforgiving – Matthew 6:14&15

Conditions to forgiveness – Luke 17:3&4

The prodigal son – Luke 15:11-24

Willingness to forgive – Matthew 6:14

'Father forgive them' – Luke 23:34

Lead us not into Temptation

Surrounded by so many dangers

Who or what can tempt us? What are the sources of temptation? From the prayer itself, logically, the first answer must be – God. God our heavenly Father may lead us into temptation. He will not entice us to do wrong. As the letter of James makes plain, our heavenly Father would never tempt us to do that which he hates. He may, however, lead us into situations where, because of our own passions or weaknesses, because of pressure from those around us or because of Satan's games, we will face strong encouragement or temptation to do wrong.

Not surprisingly, many people have stumbled over these words. How can it be that God would lead us into temptation? Surely there must be some mistake? Well, in a sense, there is. It lies in our use of old and treasured words, even when they have several shades of meaning. We will be hard pressed to find a better word than the all-embracing word 'temptation', but need to bear in mind that, acknowledging our weakness, we are asking that our heavenly Father would not bring us to times of overwhelming trial or testing.

In the sense of trials and testings, temptations can be good or they can be bad. They can so easily cause us to fall. And yet, successfully resisted, they can strengthen us and enable us to grow and live more boldly for God. In this positive sense each disciple needs to grow in ability to face temptation.

For a moment we leave the splendour of the house and step outside to the coach-houses and the stable block. Great houses have always had very extensive stables, often clustered round a straw-blown stable yard.

It is only during this last hundred years or so that motor cars and tractors have replaced horses, reducing the stabling and riding of horses to a leisure pursuit. Until then almost everyone would learn to ride, as today almost everyone learns to drive. Learning to drive or learning to ride is a risky and testing time – a time of temptation.

As a son of the house learns to ride, for example, he will first be placed in the saddle of the smallest and most dependable pony and gently led a few paces. As he grows more confident the length of the halter rope can be extended, giving him greater freedom to be in charge of the pony, until the day comes when he no longer needs to be led but can be the master of his own pony. His ability to ride has been carefully matched with the trial, danger and risk of a fall. Our heavenly Father is like that, he will allow us to be tested in order to enable us to grow, to mature.

But, there will come a time when the youngster is first allowed to ride out into the open country and onto the road. What temptation! What risk! The pony might bolt or the lad, as yet without practical experience or road sense, might gallop away in a crazy manner. Yet, unless he is allowed out of the stable yard, he will never learn to ride – and so it is with us. God is the best of fathers. His will is our ongoing growth as disciples. His aim is that we might stand strong and spiritually mature through days of temptation. We will only stand firm in such times if, before then, our heavenly Father has allowed us to grow by leading us through many times of testing and trial.

Like the best of fathers God does allow us to grow, he allows us to flex our spiritual muscles. He allows us to use the spiritual sword so that we might be prepared for spiritual warfare and stand in the day of difficulty. In this sense God, our heavenly Father, leads us into temptation.

We often admire the spiritual giants among us – but it is salutary to ask them to tell of some of the many, sore trials they have faced; the trials that have brought them to the strong and radiant faith we now so envy.

As we pray, the Lord has given us an opportunity to stop and remember that we are weak and frail and set in a fallen world, a world full of danger and hurt; physical, mental and spiritual, and to pray for God-given wisdom and protection. 'Lord watch over us; please keep us humbly aware of the dangers that surround us, growing in ability to face them, and safe. Do not let us be tested beyond the little we can stand.'

Although temptation is always an opportunity to grow in spiritual strength and maturity, it is also a snare that would cause us to stumble. Even a mature and able rider can be thrown by a slip, a stone, a branch or a frightened horse. The most mature disciple is equally vulnerable. We do need to learn to walk humbly; to pray frequently for protection, discernment, wisdom and grace. In this petition our Lord teaches us to do just that.

Temptation from the world
The world around us is our great testing ground. It cares nothing for God or godly ways. It will present us with an attractive and brightly-lit supermarket display of alternative lifestyles, faiths and world views. Like shoppers we are enticed and urged to choose for ourselves and be uncritical of the choices of others. True Christianity,

judged to have passed its sell-by date, is generally presented as a 'museum corner' of musty and outdated hymn books, damp and dark churches, strange robes and rituals that have little or no bearing on real life.

The world will also tempt us with short cuts to fame and fortune; offer to make us instant millionaires; owners of our own stately homes. It will tempt us with sharp practice in business and less than integrity in dealing with other people's money. Although the law and codes of practice aim to restrict these things, there will always be the pressure and the powerful temptation to search for loopholes or weak points in the fence of the law or places where it can be 'moved a little' for our personal or corporate gain. In business and at home we will be tempted to put ourselves first and regard everyone else as 'disposable'. Trust and honourable dealing are closely tied to godliness and so for the disciple, the Christian, this fallen world presents a whole minefield of temptation.

Temptation from within

Our own flesh will tempt us in so many ways. We will be enticed to throw off the 'inhibitions of godliness' and seek 'self-fulfilment'; self-gratification at every level. We will be tempted to be carried along by our desires, feelings and moods. Anger, resentment and 'black moods' take a conscious effort to manage in a God-honouring way, but the temptation will always be to give them free rein, to give vent to our feelings by 'taking it out' on those around us.

We will be enticed to throw off 'outdated morality', enjoy ourselves and be 'free'. Being human we will be sorely tempted to cut free from the narrow path of discipleship and join in. 'And do I not burn?' asked the apostle Paul as he speaks of another man's fall.

King David, a full-blooded warrior, sent his troops to fight while he spent an idle spring in Jerusalem. Looking out from the roof-top resting place of his royal house his eyes fell on a beautiful woman bathing – maybe she intended it to be that way. The temptation was overwhelming – and the outcome: adultery, intrigue, manslaughter and a home-life dogged with difficulty.

In the course of his duty, Joseph, as a young and handsome slave in Egypt, found himself passionately desired by his master's wife. (Here is the occupational hazard of a resident helper or 'au pair'!) For Joseph the invitations were incessant, the opportunities plentiful but, by the grace of God, he stood his ground holding his master's marriage in honour: 'Far be it from me to sin against heaven and my master.' The lady's determination and passion grew and the moment came when Joseph's priority was to get out, to escape. Says scripture, 'Flee immorality,' unashamedly run from it. If like Joseph, we find ourselves in a situation where we face overwhelming pressure to do what is wrong before the Lord God, we do well to follow Joseph's example – to get out, to escape from it, whatever the taunts or threats. For Joseph it meant prison, but under the hand of God it was also the pathway by which he was led to great usefulness. God honours those who honour him.

Spiritual warfare
Our heavenly Father is in control of all our circumstances, poverty or plenty, war or peace, life and death itself. But under his hand, the world will tempt us with its delights, privileges, possessions and power. The flesh, our own anger, passions, moods, weaknesses and inner corruptions will leave us wide open to temptation. And Satan, always in the background, will seek to play on our human weaknesses and on our circumstances for his own ends.

Behind our daily, small temptations to stray from God's holy ways lies the great temptation to rebel against God. We may be gently lured away little by little, like sheep eating one delicious patch of grass after the next, until we have strayed very far from godly ways and thinking. Or, we may come under great pressure to deny the faith and turn our back on God. In the Old Testament, the great temptation of Job to 'curse God and die' was of this nature. Pray that our heavenly Father would spare us from such terrible temptation. Pray for those imprisoned even now for their faith and enticed with the promise of 'instant freedom' if they will deny their faith and assent to some other faith, philosophy or world-view.

The great tribulation of which the New Testament warns must be of this nature; times when Satan and his servants do all in their power to seduce, crush and disinherit the saints of God.

We deceive ourselves so easily and are so blissfully unaware of the dangers in which we stand. Like little children who will just run into a road, we so easily run into a situation in which we are overwhelmed by difficulty or temptation. That is exactly what happened to the apostle Peter. Jesus had warned him that Satan would tempt him, but said Peter; 'Lord, they may all fall away, but I will stand firm even to death.' Peter did not know himself, or the overwhelming nature of temptation. He did not know the danger into which he was running. He was so sure of his own strength that he rushed into terrible testing. Then, confronted by ordinary people who identified him as one of Jesus' disciples, the great apostle totally collapsed.

However, before you condemn Peter, put yourself in his position. The Lord had been violently arrested and was facing death. The accusation is made: 'You were there. You are one of them.' How would you react? It is easy to point the finger at Peter but, if on your immediate answer, hung imprisonment or freedom, life or death, would it not appear 'wiser' to say, 'I never knew him.' The temptation is absolutely overwhelming and that is the nature of temptation. Yet, like Peter, we so easily rush into it. They were no fools who taught us to pray morning by morning, '. . . that we might fall into no sin neither run into any kind of danger.'

The world will squeeze us into its mould, the flesh is weak and vulnerable and Satan, who plays on our circumstances, whatever they are, will turn them to trip us.

If we are young we will be invited many times to join the party: 'Enjoy yourself! Break free! Just forget God and the narrow path of faith.'

If we are poor we may be sorely tempted to steal or deceive to obtain what we feel we need: 'They have so much more than I do, I have a right to take it.'

If we are fit and well we will be tempted to forget God in the whirl of sport, family, pleasure or business life.

If we are successful and rich, we will be tempted to put God out of our thinking: 'I have no longer any need of God.'

Should we fall seriously ill, we will be tempted to self-pity; to murmur against those who are looking after us: 'They do not really care. They have not noticed how terrible I feel this morning or that I need . . .' Self pity is the temptation exactly matched to those who are unwell.

The same temptation may be directed towards God – to doubt his goodness, or to doubt his power. In times of great trouble, it is easy to think, 'If God really cared would he leave me in this situation?' or, 'Is God really in control?'

There is an almost infinite variety of temptations, each presented by and hence precisely matched to, our particular situation. It is for this reason that other people's temptations are always so much easier to face than our own! Their temptations would never trip us up but our own are much more difficult. Each temptation, each time of testing, is an opportunity to grow, to make a God-honouring response – or to tumble.

The Lord Jesus is teaching disciples that we need to be aware, as Peter was so blissfully unaware, that we are frail and vulnerable and open to attack. He is teaching us to pray for courage, guidance and protection as we face each new and testing situation.

Praying for one another

Again, do notice that we are not just praying for ourselves. Here, as throughout the Lord's Prayer, it is 'us' and 'our' not 'me' and 'my'. Certainly, 'Lead me not into temptation,' as I face a particular situation or person, but also 'us' and 'our'. Families, countries, companies and churches are all being constantly tested and can all be sorely tempted. In the far reaching decisions that are made, the temptations for short-term gain, for exploitation, for worldly but ungodly ways are very great. Therefore pray that they, or we, as we play our part, may not be led into temptation, but may stand with godly integrity and courage.

Such prayers have by no means passed their sell-by date!

In the opening chapter of the Old Testament book of Job, we are shown Job praying for his family. He is praying for his sons in their eating and drinking and making merry. 'Lord God, there are so many dangers, lead them not into temptation, forgive them where they have fallen, keep them safe.' What a helpful pattern for our own praying.

The Lord himself, in the garden before his arrest urged the disciples to pray that they might not fall into temptation. He also prayed for them. 'Peter, Satan has desired to sift you as wheat is sifted, to test and tempt you very severely, but I have prayed for you'.

'But I have prayed for you.' How many of us have cause to thank God for those who prayed for us in worldly, fleshly, God-forgetting days as Satan sought to test us. I thank God for a praying grandmother who prayed – while I wandered blissfully unaware through the spiritual minefield of student days.

'Father, lead us not into temptation, we pray that you would keep us, and those we care about, safe. May we not be squeezed by the world, driven by the flesh or manipulated by Satan to do what seems so desirable in the moment, but is ungodly or ultimately destructive. Give us increasing discernment, wisdom and courage to live for you day by day.'

Questions for personal reflection or discussion

1. In what ways and to what purpose can our heavenly Father lead us into, and through, times and situations of sore temptation?
2. For the disciple of Christ, in what sense is the whole of life full of temptations?
3. How can this petition humble us and so help us to cope with our natural, spiritual pride?
4. Which particular temptations does our own society forcefully present to us?
5. Does the longing 'to be ourselves', 'to freely express and be the person our genes or environment would make us', need to be brought under the control of our Lord's call to holiness of living; of obedience and of taking up our cross daily and following him?

6. Joseph, pursued by his master's wife, had to make a costly decision – the cost of earning the lady's scorn and anger, or the far greater cost of knowingly disobeying the Lord God and betraying his master's trust. Might we have to make an equally costly decision, if for example, we are pressured by our friends to steal or to take drugs, or by our employer to deceive?
7. Does God still honour those who honour him?
8. Strong and blustering Peter rushed into terrible temptation – would we have done any better if we had been in his situation?
9. Why are other people's temptations no great problem to us, when our own are so difficult?
10. In what ways does it help us if we recognise that, despite our apparent self-reliance and strength, we are actually frail and vulnerable and open to attack?
11. What value is there in praying for our friends, our families and for one another that we do not fall into temptation?

References

God tempts no one – James 1:13
'Curse God' – Job 1:11, 2:5 & 2:9
The great tribulation – Matthew 24:21 and Revelation 7:13-17
'And do I not burn' (passion or indignation) – 2 Corinthians 11:29
David tempted – 2 Samuel 11:2-5
Joseph tempted – Genesis 39:6-20
'Flee immorality' – 1 Corinthians 6:18
Those who honour him – 1 Samuel 2:30
Jesus warning Peter – Luke 22:31-34
Peter's temptation – Luke 22:55-62
Job and his family – Job 1:4&5
'To sift you as wheat' – Luke 22:31

Keep us, Deliver us from Evil

Safety in an evil world

We live in a world that is at the same time glorious and tragic. It is a wonderful world with so much that is noble, pure and breathtakingly beautiful; but it is also a fallen world, a world shot through with suffering and injustice, malice and evil. God our heavenly Father understands the evil we face as does our Lord who taught us to pray these words.

The Lord of Glory humbled himself and came among us. He shared our life, experienced the pain of rejection, hatred and grave injustice; he faced the most excruciating death in order to free us from the grip and power of evil.

Hell is the ultimate evil and our heavenly Father knows, as we do not, its depth and its horror. He gave his only Son to rescue us from that ultimate evil. God our heavenly Father is the great deliverer, our Saviour.

Despite their loveliness great houses have always been open to all kinds of troubles; to troubles from within, from members of the family itself or from those employed in the running of the house, among whom may be those who would deceive, steal or even destroy the household. They are also open to troubles from without, from people who would break in and help themselves to treasures, antiques or important papers, and from those who would break in to kidnap, hurt or destroy.

In the kingdom of heaven, as with a great house, our happiness and our security lie in knowing the dangers we face, and in being watchful and on our guard. So, from the warmth and wonder of our heavenly Father's goodness to us and purposes for us, we must turn to be forewarned of the evil depths of our own hearts, of the sheer hatred of evil people and of the malice and cunning of Satan.

The prayer, 'Deliver us from evil,' is consistently found in the texts of the gospel of Matthew and expands the previous petition. We have prayed that we might not be led into overwhelmingly evil situations, now we pray for protection and for deliverance within them.

Firstly, our Lord taught us to plead for rescue from the evil thoughts, words and deeds that are conceived, spoken and done almost before we realise what is happening.

Deliver us from evil thinking.
It was the great German reformer Martin Luther who taught us that we cannot stop the birds flying over our heads, but we can stop them nesting in our hair!

It is the nature of these brilliant things we call our brains to be constantly turning over all kinds of ideas, often quite unconsciously. All sorts of ideas 'just arrive' but it is our responsibility before our heavenly Father to either develop them or expel them. Brilliant ideas and useless ideas; wonderful, godly and selfless ideas or vile, evil and destructive ideas are constantly entering our conscious minds either to be enjoyed, delighted in and turned into action; or to be rejected and thrown out.

These ideas are inspired by all that we see, hear and feel. They are inspired by our present situation or by the lovely or terrible experiences of the past; inspired by our heavenly Father or thrown in like a hand grenade by the evil one to wreak destruction. However they arrive, the kind of ideas presented by our sub-conscious minds will be influenced by what we feed into them and by what we welcome from them.

The kind of birds overhead depends on where we choose to walk. Walk in the country in the early morning and you may well be greeted by the skylark, walk in the city square and mind the pigeons, walk by the coast and watch the gulls wheel and swoop over your head. In the same way the kind of ideas that flood into our minds depends on where we put ourselves. They are influenced by the people with whom we associate, the magazines and papers we read, the films and programmes we watch. All these will influence the ideas that flood into our minds. If you throw bread in the city, you are inviting the pigeons to settle. If you throw bread at the coast, the gulls will be around you in less than a moment.

We may actively choose to restrict our conscious thinking to all that is good, honourable and worthy of praise, as the apostle Paul urges us to. Alternatively, we may invite other 'birds' to settle. For example, we may welcome and revel in very negative and destructive thoughts about ourselves or about those around us. How many of the difficulties in our relationships with one another flow from allowing thoughts like these to grow and develop!

By our choice of cinema, television, video and computer viewing our sub-conscious minds are flooded with very powerful images for good – or for evil. We live in days when we watch and regard as 'entertainment' violence, vice and evil, but are horrified when people put the very fantasies we enjoy into practice in the real world.

At this more dramatic level, we may 'so throw our bread' as to encourage our sub-conscious minds to supply us with unrestrained fantasies of financial or political power, of sex or of violent revenge. They will respond accordingly, supplying ideas to achieve our chosen end, be it fraud, rape or nuclear warfare!

The potential is within each of us, for out of the heart comes all that is pure, noble and lovely but out of the heart comes also every evil thought: unkindness, uncleanness, theft, envy and murder. All these come from within. Both Judas' betrayal of his Lord and Hitler's 'final solution', the extermination of the Jewish people were, once, 'just a thought.'

'Lord, deliver us from evil thinking, rescue us from feeding on and revelling in that which is evil. Wake us up so that we may recognise the poison of evil thinking for what it is. Give us strength, despite its fascination, to turn it off, kick it out, to scare away such 'birds', before they 'nest', bringing havoc to our homes, our lives or our society – Father, keep us from evil.'

Deliver us from evil speaking.
A retired missionary was telling how the Lord first challenged him. As a lad of sixteen, he was with his friends on a train. They were 'proving their manhood' by loudly outdoing one another in foul language. A man in the corner was totally ignored but, as he left the carriage, he very quietly said to the future missionary, 'Young man, if your heart is as evil as your mouth, you are in very great trouble.'

From our lips escape all too easily all kinds of evil: words that are lying or deceitful; words that crush and destroy; words that are foul or words that throw into the gutter something that is lovely or holy.

How many relationships are destroyed by an unrecognised habit of evil speaking! We are commanded to love and build-up one another, and yet self-centred, arrogant, critical and destructive words so easily escape our lips: 'What is the matter with you!' 'You've done it again!' 'You're useless!' or in their absence, 'He'll never be any good!' 'He's rubbish!'

'Lord set a guard on our lips, keep us from evil speaking – to one another, and of one another.'

Deliver us from evil deeds.
Evil deeds may be done for all kinds of hidden reasons. We may be blinded to what we are doing by sickness, by the heat of lust, by anger or by an all consuming commitment to a cause. In lust and in anger we only think of ourselves. In the total devotion to a political, racial or religious cause it is all too easy to lay aside the godly principles of kindness, courtesy, justice, mercy and good will. We assume that belonging to our group gives us the right to treat other groups of people with contempt. We do to them what we would not like done to ourselves.

The Lord warned his disciples that they would be persecuted and even put to death by men who were really convinced that they were doing it 'for God'. St. Paul was such a man when, as Saul the zealous Pharisee, he persecuted the Christian believers. Many a man, like Saul, has done terrible evil, believing it to be right, because he has done it for a political or religious 'cause'. Harshness, hatred and persecution, beatings, burnings, imprisonments, shootings and bombings – 'Father, keep us from evil.'

In the partnership of godly marriage our heavenly Father has provided the right setting to find human fulfilment at every level. Biologically, the sexual drive is like a fire. In the hearth or boiler of our home it can give warmth and comfort, whilst outside of godly marriage, it can burn like a fire out of control, raging and driving all before it. Unchecked and unmanaged, our sexual urge and lust can drive us to all kinds of evil. It can lead to all sorts of ungodly partnerships; to unfaithfulness within marriage and to the breaking of other homes and marriages by adultery. In the extreme, it can lead to perversion or child abuse. Here is a prayer that we may face our sexual nature and so channel it that it burns only in the God-given hearth of the marriage partnership and does not become a force for evil, destroying our own and other people's lives.

Closely linked is that other wild horse, anger. Anger is the characteristic of the young man which, wild and untamed, leads to so much hurt and destruction. However, 'broken-in' and under control it can enable us to stand with strong and godly passion against oppression and evil. It was in godly anger that the Lord cleared the temple of thieving money-changers and crooked salesmen who had made the house of prayer a den of thieves. It was with godly passion that William Wilberforce and his colleagues fought for the abolition of slavery. It is this kind of godly anger that has driven all the great social reformers.

We are social creatures and strongly need to belong to an organisation or group of friends. However, it is too easy to link with a group where the pressure from our peers is to do wrong, to do evil. In youth it is so easy to be swept into heavy drinking, the misuse of drugs etc.

To provide for our social need, our heavenly Father has given us a 'gang' or family. It is the fellowship of his church and in it, despite its many imperfections, we are called to care about one another, to encourage one another in holiness of living and to work as a team for his kingdom.

Holiness of living and true discipleship are all about bringing our natural and biological inclinations, desires and lusts under the lordship of Christ. It is a matter of putting to death or denying ourselves all that our Father hates, or, as our Lord so memorably put it, of taking up our cross daily and following him.

'Lord God, give us grace and patience to bring our driving passions under your control. Keep us from evil thinking, evil speaking and evil deeds.'

Secondly, our Lord taught us to plead for rescue from evil from without; to pray for rescue from evil people, evil days and from the evil one.

Deliver us from evil men and women.
The driving force behind the desire for leadership is the desire for power; power over people, power to influence and change lives, power to rule and direct. Like so many things, such power is two edged, it can be channelled and used for great good or it can be used for great evil. Here is a prayer that our heavenly Father would keep us from using the authority entrusted to us in our homes, at our work, or in the wider society, in a way that is evil. It is also a prayer that he would keep us safe from those who are using a position of power for evil.

Evil at home turns the place of love and safety into a prison house of fear, violence and abuse. At work, an evil 'boss', shop steward or group turns a place of creativity into a place of stress and abuse at every level.

In the church evil men, 'wolves' as both our Lord and the apostle Paul call them, may be charming, eloquent and persuasive as they gain power over us, 'relieve' us of our money or lead us astray morally or theologically.

In society, where at its best we support and encourage one another, how unthinkably terrible it is to come under the power of terrorists or to be under a death threat from evil religious extremists, caught up by a violent gang, or hemmed in by an organised crime ring. We do well to thank God daily if we know nothing of such things and to pray that he would keep us safe. We need to cry to God daily if we find ourselves, or know of fellow disciples, trapped by such evil, at home, at work or in the wider society.

Sometimes, 'Deliver us from evil' will be a cry for godly wisdom, strength and protection within a terrible situation. Sometimes it will be a prayer for courage and a godly way of escape, for the New Testament unashamedly urges us to escape from evil oppression. Sometimes it will be a prayer for those we know who are caught up in evil.

Sometimes this prayer will be a cry from the heart as far-reaching, perhaps national, choices, decisions and appointments are made. 'Lord, spare us from evil leaders and from evil laws.' For nationally, too, we do well to pray that our heavenly Father would keep us from evil.

In the wider world, from time to time, evil men rise up and create havoc – war, great suffering and destruction. How terrible it was for godly men and women to be caught up under Hitler and the Nazi regime on the far right of politics, or under Stalin and the Communists on the far left. How almost impossibly hard it is for a Christian, especially for a Christian leader, to live for the Lord under an evil and oppressive regime, be it atheistic or religious. 'Lord, deliver us . . .'

'Father, deliver us.' can also be a cry, from within an evil situation, to deliver us from the natural anger, resentment and malice that wells up in our own hearts towards those who threaten and abuse us – this in itself is an evil that would destroy us. From the prison camps have come many accounts of those who, by the grace of God, have learned to rise above the malice and hatred of the camp and be free before God to pray for, and even to love, those who taunted and persecuted and imprisoned them.

'Lord, deliver us from evil men and women in positions of power, and from our own ungodly response to the evil we experience in our day by day living.'

Lord, deliver us from, and in, the evil day.
The evil day is the day of personal or social calamity. It is the day we hear from the doctor that our remaining days are very short. It is the day we learn the terrible truth of trust betrayed, or witness the sudden death of those we had loved with all our heart.

Although we must walk through the valley of the shadow of death, it is the promise of our heavenly Father to walk with us. We need fear no evil. Nevertheless we are taught to pray that our Father would spare us from such overwhelming evil.

Evil days can touch a whole nation; days of financial ruin, days of famine or the unthinkably dreadful days of war with the accompanying loss of home, loss of loved ones, loss of everything. The whole book of Job wrestles with such evil days; days of utter calamity.

The book of Job also shows us that behind such days can be very evil forces. As we pray, 'Keep us from evil,' it is also right to pray, 'Keep us, deliver us, from the evil one.'

The Lord's Prayer is not about sweet sentiment. It is about the glorious and terrible reality of living for our heavenly Father in this fallen and often evil world. It is an essential prayer for safety and deliverance for ourselves, our families, our land and our fellow disciples throughout the world.

'Father we thank you for every day that you spare us from evil; evil that, in this fallen world, may touch our lives at any time. Help us to use the good days you give us for the honour of your name, and walk closely with us through the dark days. By your grace, bring us safely through them.'

Questions for personal reflection or discussion

Our thoughts
1. How might we feel if all the thoughts that pass through our minds were known to those around us?
2. What kind of negative and destructive thoughts, allowed to grow and develop, might harm ourselves, our home lives or our working relationships?
3. How do we feed our minds? How do we regard the fantasy world of the magazine, television or computer?
4. How can we control what we think about?

Our words
1. How evil are our mouths? Do we cheapen godly or precious things by the way in which we speak?
2. Do we use our words to encourage and build up – or to undermine, crush or destroy?

Our deeds
1. Saul persecuted the early Christian believers out of religious zeal. Are there people who we despise or treat unfairly? How can we keep ourselves from such evil?
2. Can strong attractions lead us to immorality? What has our heavenly Father provided to be the right place for passionate love and to keep us from such evil?
3. Can anger ever be right?
  What good can come from anger?
  What evil can come from anger?
  Can you name some examples?

Other people
1. Can you think of examples in which people have used their power a) for great good, or, b) for great evil?
2. How can we best help our fellow Christians stand firm under the present, increasingly aggressive tide of atheistic secularism that is sweeping the West, where we are under threat if we think or say anything other than what is considered to be 'politically correct'?
3. How much are we aware or concerned about our fellow disciples abroad who are being evilly oppressed? Could these things happen here?
4. How natural is it to return evil for evil, hatred for hatred? How can we begin to cope?

Evil days
1. Why and how can evil days of war and want, of financial collapse or of serious illness, narrow our vision of living in God's world in a way that brings honour to him?

Footnote

Keep us from evil – the part that is ours to play
It was famously said by U.S. President Thomas Jefferson, among others, that the price of freedom is eternal vigilance. The saying clearly applies to those called to positions of government, whose task it is to protect and look after our society both nationally and internationally.

As constant vigilance applies on the national scale, so it also applies personally to our own safety and the safety of those for whom we are responsible; at home, in our work situation and in the places where we meet. A local shop keeper, speaking of protecting his customers from hurt and his stock from theft, simply quoted these same words 'eternal vigilance'.

References

'Good, honourable' etc. – Philippians 4:8
'Theft, murder, envy' etc. – Mark 7:21-23
Murder, 'for God' – John 16:1-3
Saul persecuting Christian believers – Acts 8:1-3 and 1 Timothy 1:12-15
Clearing the temple – Luke 19:45&46
Group pressure to do evil, a warning – Exodus 23:2
'Wolves' – Matthew 7:15, Acts 20:29, 2 Peter 2:1-3
Escape evil oppression – Mark 13:14
With us in the valley of the shadow – Psalm 23

Deliver us from Evil, continued

The one who would deceive and destroy

A heart that readily wells up with evil ideas and plans, flesh that delights in them, a fallen world that brings to us all kinds of evil days, people, circumstances and opportunities – and in the shadows, hiding behind all these things is Satan, the evil one. In scripture he is also described as the deceiver and the destroyer. In the Lord's Prayer it is legitimate to translate, 'Deliver us from evil,' 'Deliver us from the evil one.' We do not only wrestle with flesh and blood, but with mighty, deceptive and destructive spiritual forces under the evil one.

We are guests in our heavenly Father's world and yet Satan, a fallen servant of God, will constantly suggest, as he did at the first, that God's commands are irksome and restricting; that our heavenly Father is denying us a basic 'right', namely, to do as we will, to be as gods. He tempts us to break free from God and do as we will. Here is Satan's basic ploy. See how he uses it again and again.

Satan and society
The prophet Isaiah reminds us that, 'a people's . . . greatest treasure is their reverence for the Lord.'

In modern Western culture, with our great Christian heritage, perhaps the most effective way in which the evil one has been at work is by way of post-modern, secular, humanist thinking. Here is a way of thinking that cuts free from God and his fatherly commands and instructions. The underlying assumption, often unspoken, is that we don't need to take account of God; we can forget him, be as gods and so do as we choose. By it Satan has been able to bring our godly heritage all but tumbling down.

Successive governments have laid aside godly moral values, and replaced them with a whole sea of relative values. These are human values that simply depend on current social thinking, the circumstances in which we find ourselves, the effectiveness of a pressure group or on the whim of the ruling political party. Such thinking is always presented very plausibly and forcefully and yet it has exposed us to a flood of evil right across our society.

In Britain, post-modern thinking underlies the throwing off of godly ways and a sliding back into old and pagan ways right across the moral spectrum. Godly chastity before marriage and faithfulness within it are displaced by a widespread thinking which regards the exclusive and lifelong commitment of marriage as of little importance, relatively stable partnerships becoming the normal pattern. It is a way of thinking that can lead to the collapse of godly family life, and ultimately to the collapse of society.

How far will we slide? Roman society women dated the year by the name of the then current partner. Indeed, many ancient Romans sought any partner, homosexual or heterosexual, at any time – with children of mixed parentage loosely attached along the way. However, for our encouragement, this was the very cradle or seedbed of the New Testament church.

In the freshly planted churches of the Roman Empire, Christian disciples were a people with a new and distinctive way of living. However, the effect in our own days of declining godliness is, firstly, to make appear 'very odd' those Christian disciples still living our heavenly Father's narrow but best way and, secondly, to alienate great swathes of people, who have nothing against the Christian church, but find themselves excluded from it by the way in which they have been encouraged to live.

There is a very great social cost attached to the prevailing godless way of thinking. It has undermined the family, offering 'equally valid' alternative lifestyles, but they are lifestyles that tend to the breaking down of society as a whole. These ungodly lifestyles have produced, often not of their own choosing, many more single parents and homeless teenagers. This flows from the casual nature of modern parenting partnerships where one or the other partner may move on or 'be replaced' and youngsters find that the new relationship in some way excludes them. This casual approach has also given us a spiralling tax burden that the rest of society must pay to care for many who are no longer in, what are amazingly economically efficient, mutually supporting family groups.

This tide of secular thinking has also destroyed so much that was orderly, good and godly in the education of our young people. It has added to godly honest dealing a range of 'creative' financial approaches. It has brought into medicine what is in practice abortion on demand, the 'right' to destroy a dependent life that is not wanted; a way of thinking naturally to be extended to euthanasia. It has filled our society with groups demanding rights of every kind, and has largely taken away the sense of personal and social responsibility so that what might be described as 'subsidised irresponsibility' flourishes.

In short, ungodly, post-modern, liberal thinking has brought with it a whole rising tide of evil. And most sinister of all, it lays out a 'red carpet' for the advance of strong and determined alien cultures. Cultures which across the world, while often claiming to be victim, consistently deceive, threaten and crush with violence all that stands in the way of their advance and in particular crush godliness and godly people.

Behind all this, Satan smiles as deceit and destruction flourish and the godly foundations of our law-abiding society are steadily undermined.

For many years our heavenly Father has protected this country from evil, surrounded it and kept it safe, but how can we expect the continued blessing of God in this privileged way and yet turn our back on him? Disciples of Christ need earnestly to pray, 'Keep us from evil.' 'Deliver us from the evil ways and evil influences to which we as a nation, in our God-forgetting and all-tolerant way, have laid ourselves wide open.'

Satan and the church
Within the church the strategies of the evil one have been equally effective. By the same ungodly post-modern thinking, he has undermined true faith in great sections of the church, offering well-presented human teaching which displaces the teaching of our Lord and of his apostles. By this thinking, for example, he is tearing apart the church over the heart of Christian belief; the person and work of the Lord Jesus Christ, his deity and the significance of his cross and resurrection. And over practical issues such as the spiritual headship of women, and the acceptability of homosexual practice.

In our worship, Satan, the deceiver, delights to replace sincerity of heart and holiness of living with splendour of ceremony or with heat of emotion.

In our fellowships, at every opportunity, Satan, the destroyer, sows those fast-growing weeds of mistrust, discord and envy. How we need to be constantly on our guard, praying that, '. . . we may agree in the truth of God's holy word and live in godly love and unity'; testing all we hear and read against the plain teaching of scripture, and actively guarding our fellowship with one another. Satan delights both to lead us astray and to divide us. He delights to see the church, at the local, national and international level, destroying itself.

Satan and ourselves
Satan is the master of his art. His constant aim is to cause us to stumble. Behind Job's terrible trials was Satan seeking to cause Job to curse God to his face. Behind Peter's terrible night, as he found himself denying his Lord, was Satan seeking to cause Peter to fall. Yet on the surface, all could be accounted for by personal weaknesses, by the pressure and persuasion of the people around them or by the circumstances in which they found themselves.

The evil one plays on our anxieties, fears and hardness of heart in order to undermine or destroy our walk with our heavenly Father and our walk with our fellow disciples. This world really is a spiritual mine-field!

Satan works indirectly through material wealth, pleasure, anxiety or the pressures of life, to make us forgetful, fruitless and cold towards the things of God. It is for these reasons that it is so hard for the successful person, modern and materialistic, to enter the kingdom of heaven. It is for these reasons that young Christian disciples, who begin so full of vision and passion for God, so often end up in middle-life cold, indifferent and fruitless. 'Father, keep us from evil.'

Satan works more directly as the destroyer as he presents ideas and convictions that would wreck our walk with our heavenly Father or our usefulness in his service. The recorded temptations of our Lord are exactly of this pattern. Each, though presented as apparently highly desirable, would have either destroyed him or his work. He was tempted to use his authority and power for his own gratification; at that moment to satisfy his hunger. He was tempted to commit a spectacular suicide and so destroy himself. And finally he was tempted, in the privacy of the moment, to gain all – with ease – at the price of becoming a double agent, a secret servant of Satan.

We can face similar times of testing. For us, the temptations of Satan can be presented as the persuasive argument of a false shepherd or of an atheist, the advice of a 'friend', or simply a 'gut feeling'.

More rarely, but dramatically, Satan works as the destroyer through tricks of the mind. He is sometimes behind quite overwhelming and terrifying thoughts of destruction, both of ourselves and of those around us; fiery darts indeed, to be recognised by their sudden force and destructiveness. Our heavenly Father does not shout at us! So if, when you are under great stress, depressed or just very tired, you feel a strong prompting to, 'Finish it all, throw yourself in front of this train,' – hold fast. If it is, 'I could kill you,' – hold fast. If it is, 'Drive into the ditch, now,' – keep steady. Or, in the early hours you might wake from a dream with a mind filled with the most unthinkable scenes of violence or vice, from which you recoil in horror. Such things are by no means uncommon, but they are not of God. 'Lord, deliver us from evil. Keep us safe, keep us steady.'

Even more directly, if we have in some way played into Satan's hands, we may find ourselves or come across others who are directly under the influence, or even control of the evil one. We can so easily bite on his bait for it is always presented so attractively. As a former generation put it, 'Satan's delicacies are always served on silver salvers.' It is so desirable to know the future; to have hidden powers; to be in touch with the spirits; to be in contact with those we have lost through death. Yet to pursue any of these is to bite on Satan's bait. Can this also be a hidden danger behind an invitation to join a secret brotherhood or lodge, or even behind certain job or financial offers?

We are involved in spiritual warfare where powerful spiritual agencies would enthral us, ensnare us and enlist us for their own ends and purposes. They may offer us 'the world', as Satan offered our Lord. They may offer all we could desire as Satan offered in the Garden of Eden, but the aim is always to lure us from single hearted loyalty to our heavenly Father.

In the early chapters of Genesis we read that, after their disobedience, their fall, both the man and the woman tried to hide themselves from God. After such an encounter with Satan's temptation, whether we fall or not, it takes very great courage to come to our heavenly Father in honest and open confession. And yet our Father does not look on the outward appearance, but on the heart. In the kingdom of heaven there are no hidden secrets and there are no double agents.

If we have been caught by the evil one we need to cry to our heavenly Father for mercy. Deliverance and forgiveness are freely available; they have been purchased for us by the cross, the precious death, of the Son of God, the Lord Jesus Christ. To be given them demands very courageous openness with our heavenly Father, from whom nothing is hidden. It takes great courage, but, for those who dare, for those who come to him hiding nothing, he has promised forgiveness, deliverance and a fresh new start. The wonderful truth is that there are no depths of evil into which we may fall, from which the grace of God in our Lord Jesus Christ cannot rescue us.

'Father, spare us, rescue us from the evil we have brought on ourselves. Keep us watchful and safe from the evil one with all his subtlety and with all his skill. Turn us again, as leaders and people, to hunger after that which is just and godly, and to stand against that which is evil. Cause your name to be honoured, your kingdom to come and your will to be done.'

Questions for personal reflection or discussion

1. To what extent does Satan keep in the shadows?
2. Why do moral values that are not anchored to godliness drift? What anchor has God our Father given us?
3. Why will true disciples appear increasingly 'odd' in an ungodly society?
4. Why might it encourage us to know that the ancient Roman Empire was the seed bed of the Christian church?
5. In what ways does ungodly thinking undermine the family? Resulting from this, what are the costs, of different kinds, to be borne by the children, the wider family, the community and the state?
6. In what ways have you seen Satan play the secret destroyer among disciples in the church?

More personal questions
1. Do we need to be watchful? For what kinds of things, situations or people?

2. How can evil creep up on us until we are all but spiritually dead, or at least fruitless?

3. Do we need to be personally aware and praying much more for one another – that we may recognise and resist Satan's fiery darts?

4. In what ways might we play into Satan's hands?

5. How will the fact that true disciples are caught up in spiritual warfare affect the way in which we live?

6. No matter how small or how great they are, why is it so hard to honestly bring our mistakes and failings to our heavenly Father – even when we know there are no secrets hidden from him?

7. What encouragement is given to come before Almighty God with complete honesty in the first chapter of the first letter of John verses 5-10?

References

Greatest treasure – Isaiah 33:6 (Today's English Version)
Wrestling with mighty spiritual forces – Ephesians 6:12
Satan behind Job's temptation to curse God – Job 1:9-11
Satan behind Peter's denial of his Lord – Luke 22:31-34
Satan behind the temptations of our Lord – Matthew 4:1-11
Warning to Peter – Luke 22:39-46
God looks on the heart – 1 Samuel 16:7
Forgiveness, deliverance and a fresh new start – 1John 1:5-10

The Kingdom, the Power and the Glory

A concluding peal of praise

Our Lord's pattern is the Hebrew pattern of prayer and worship kept together. The petitions are balanced and strengthened by reminding ourselves of the power and glory of our heavenly Father. Having just looked at the great dangers and evils that surround us, we have every reason to be weighed down. And so how good it is to turn our eyes heavenward and boldly affirm the glorious truth that our heavenly Father is the sovereign Lord; to him belong all power and glory. He is well able to rescue us, deliver us, and keep us safe even though we walk, maybe often, through the valley of the shadow of death.

One of the characteristics of stately homes is their balance, their symmetry. If one wing was never built, or was lost by the ravages of fire or dry rot, the whole building is left out of balance; half missing. Similarly with prayer, if we fail to remind ourselves of the greatness of God in praise and adoration we shall be spiritually cast down by life's great challenges, difficulties and battles. We may also become prey to a dryness of spirit which reduces prayer, and indeed the whole of our Christian living, to an unlovely, formal duty, something which has to be done and yet which has within it no contagious, God-centred joy and gladness.

On the other hand, if the aspect of heartfelt petition for this fallen world is lost we may enjoy 'praise and worship' which is quite literally out of this world. But it will be in a compartment on its own – stirring, heart-warming, deeply moving at the time and yet having little or no relevance to the reality of living in this world for God.

In public worship and in private prayer, therefore, plead with the Lord from a full heart about all the practical issues of living and revel in the fact that he is able to keep us from falling, able to present us faultless, able to do more than we can even begin to think or imagine – the kingdom, the power and ultimately all glory belong to the Lord God, our heavenly Father.

Here is a peal of praise giving glory to God our heavenly Father whose sovereign power will never cease, even forever and ever. 'The Lord God reigns. Amen, Amen.'

The little Hebrew word 'amen' so often thought of and used as if it were a 'religious full-stop' is in reality far greater. It means 'certainly so' or 'let it be so' and gives us the opportunity to 'sign our name', and add our own voice to the great affirmations and petitions of this most wonderful of prayers.

'. . . the kingdom, and the power, and the glory.' The Authorised King James Version concludes the Lord's Prayer with this magnificent ending. It is fitting and part of our godly heritage. However, many of the modern versions conclude the Lord's Prayer without this ending.

Within the services of the Church of England we use both forms of the Lord's Prayer. I used to feel we were 'given short measure' if the prayer ended with, 'Deliver us from evil.' It felt unfinished; as if, as visitors, we had been suddenly ushered from a great house having been shown just a few of the magnificent rooms! However, it is in fact a fair reflection of what we find in the New Testament.

If you study the various ancient manuscripts from which our New Testament has come, you find that not all of them have the fuller ending. Many texts stop short, ending with, 'Lead us not into temptation,' or, 'Keep us from evil,' or even earlier. There is clearly some uncertainty about the conclusion of the prayer. The traditional ending could be original or could have been something which the apostles, or early Christians, added as they came to pray it. As they prayed they came back to thinking about our heavenly Father and the great themes of this prayer and ended, surely rightly, on this note of praise, giving glory to Almighty God.

This concluding peal of praise is absolutely consistent with the earlier part of the prayer and with the whole teaching of the scriptures. It is a telling forth of who God is; the one true God who is the king of the universe. Although around us men and women ignore him, although there are many who live in active rebellion against him, we affirm that God, the living God, is Lord. Let all the earth know that the one, living God reigns.

You might ask, 'Is such a statement of the sovereignty of God a charitable, a "Christian", attitude?' We live in a very tolerant age and surely the spirit of Christianity is to be tolerant. Clearly, there is a place for tolerance, but when tolerance, gentleness with those around us, leads us to suppress the truth, then surely the principle of tolerance has led us to overthrow something far greater, far more important. It has led us to overthrow truth itself.

It is as if there were a fire at a great house and a servant went to bring a young son out of the house, but the lad said, 'No, no, leave me alone. I want to sleep; I don't want to come out.' The servant would have to say, 'I am sorry but you must come out. There is no choice, because there is something greater at stake – your own life, and that is much more important than sleep.' If we allow tolerance to overthrow truth we shall be in great trouble. This is the particular danger in which we find ourselves in our own post-modern, liberal, tolerant day. We are called by God to be his heralds, to proclaim the gospel, and yet we find ourselves squeezed by the world into being so tolerant and gracious, that we cease even to affirm that to God, and to God alone, belong the kingdom and the power and the glory.

'Brothers,' says the apostle Paul, 'pray for me that I may speak boldly as I ought to speak.' Here is a prayer worthy of echoing both for ourselves and for our Christian leaders in a world that increasingly tolerates almost anything – except the call to bow the knee to the one true God; the God and Father of our Lord Jesus Christ.

Every great house has one or two particularly fine views; views that display the estate, the gardens and the house to their very best advantage. As we conclude the Lord's Prayer we are given such a view. 'The kingdom, the power and the glory.' words which tell out the sovereign glory of the living God our heavenly Father. There is no other with whom to compare him. His alone is the kingdom, the power, and the glory. The words themselves take us back to the heart and focus of the prayer, to the three great state rooms: the honour of his name, the coming of his kingdom and the doing of his will.

This traditional ending is, as it were, a stepping back to take in the whole view of the great house in its setting. In a phrase it sets before us the whole vista of God's glory and purposes for this world. Like the flag, the royal standard, flying above a stately home, it is there to affirm that the Lord is King and that the Lord is in residence.

To him be ascribed all honour, power and glory.

> *The Lord is King! Who then shall dare*
> *Resist his will, distrust his care,*
> *Or murmur at his wise decrees,*
> *Or doubt his royal promises?*
>   Josiah Conder

Questions for personal reflection or discussion

1. Have you known churches or been through times yourself when either, a) Christian living was reduced to a dull duty, or, b) the easy words on our lips bore no relation to the tough and real world in which we live?
2. How can we keep the right balance between stirring Christian worship and practical Christian living?
3. Is the word 'amen' just a religious 'full-stop' or an opportunity for something much more?
4. The apostle John speaks of our Lord as 'full of grace and truth'. How can we keep this balance in a world that requires us to be so tolerant as to allow falsehood side by side with truth or even demands that we suppress the truth?
5. In what ways do these concluding words help us to focus on the sovereignty and purposes of God our heavenly Father?

References

'Able to keep us from falling' – Jude 24&25
The Lord God reigns – Revelation 19:6
'That I may speak boldly' – Ephesians 6:20
'Full of grace and truth' – John 1:14

The Whole Prayer in Practical Use

The great sweep of human history, or the details of one person or situation

In the life of a stately home, the business of the whole house can be directed to the general well-being of the whole estate or it can, on occasion, be focused on a single event or person. From time to time there will be activity in every room in preparation for a great occasion, an important meeting, or a family wedding or celebration. On another occasion the whole household will be going about their ordinary business but with a particular hush and concern for one member of the household who lies very ill.

As it is with a great house, so it is with the Lord's Prayer. For example:

We can pray each petition generally as we pray for the world and its leaders, and for all God's people as, together, we strive to live for him in this spiritually hostile world.

On another occasion we might first bring a whole series of concerns in our prayers and then 'gather' them as we pray the Lord's Prayer.

Following a prayer of confession, the Lord's Prayer can be a response of faith and a plea for grace and courage to start afresh to live in a way that pleases our heavenly Father.

Or we can cry to God for a particular person or situation using and applying each of the petitions in turn. The whole prayer can be focused and brought to bear, for example, on a particular meeting, or on a particular person in physical or spiritual need or on particular members of our own family.

As an example of this last and, perhaps, less usual use of the prayer, praying for a son or daughter of the house approaching marriage, we might follow each petition of the Lord's Prayer and pray:

'Father we place into your hands this couple as they approach marriage.

Cause us all to seek that your name is honoured on their wedding day, in all that is said and done in the service and in the celebrations that follow.

May they seek the honour of your name in their relationship with one another as they prepare for marriage and as they build their home together.

May your kingdom come; may they, together, submit to your holy rule and live in a way that pleases you.

May your will be done in every detail of the great day and in each decision of the months and years that lie ahead; cause there to be a touch of heaven about this marriage.

Give them day by day godly wisdom, peace and all that they need in order that they may live without anxiety before you.

Be merciful to them and grant them each a forgiving spirit towards one another that, as they adjust and settle to married life, they may be as generously forgiving – as you are towards us.

Grant them grace to withstand the particular temptations that will come to them, and from would-be suitors who would break the marriage.

Finally, Father, we ask you to protect them from every kind of evil; evil from within and evil from without, and from every onslaught of the evil one.

Cause your holy name to be held high in this marriage, Sovereign Lord, King of kings.'

Or, maybe, approaching a Christian meeting we might pray:

'Father, cause us to long that your name is held high, honoured, in our music and teaching and in all that takes place.

By your Holy Spirit, take the speaker's words and set our hearts ablaze for you, may lives be changed, may your kingdom come.

Father, we commend to you all the practical arrangements; our individual tasks and our working together. May your will be done in every detail; cause there to be a touch of heaven about this meeting.'

And so on, until we pray:

'And Father, keep us safe tonight from any who would disrupt and spoil the meeting, and from the spiritual coldness, deadness, attacks and interference of the evil one.'

Would to God that our national and local elections, great Senate and Parliamentary debates, council, governor and board meetings, synods, church meetings and individual opportunities to speak for the Lord were covered and supported by prayers like these – prayers after our Lord's pattern; prayers that we can be confident he will hear. We make up our own prayers after the 'God bless . . .' pattern, or read set prayers, but, to our great loss, we neglect this great pattern prayer of the Lord.

'Lord, open our eyes to see the armoury that you have provided for our spiritual warfare. Help us to take hold of it, understand it and use it for the honour of your holy name.'

Questions for personal reflection or discussion

1. Sometimes we will bring a whole series of concerns in our prayers and then 'gather' them as we pray the Lord's Prayer. Are you happy to use it in this way?
2. Sometimes the Lord's Prayer will be a fitting response of faith and determination after a prayer of confession. Are you comfortable with that?
3. Sometimes it will be focussed on a single issue. For example, think how each petition in turn, i.e. the whole of the Lord's Prayer, could be relevantly applied to one, or a selection, of the following situations:

    When praying for our political leaders.
    When praying for our national or local church.
    When praying for a known missionary.
    When praying for a known person in need or sickness

The Lord's Prayer Spelled Out

An extended paraphrase

Almighty and merciful heavenly Father, by invitation of your Son, we plead with you:

To cause your holy name to be held high; held in honour, feared with a holy fear and held in reverence.

To cause your kingdom to come; all of us willingly and gladly living in submission to you, under your rule, according to your commandments and fatherly instruction – working together in harmony with one another and in harmony with this beautiful planet on which you have set us, to live for the praise of your glory.

To cause your will to be done throughout the earth in the manner in which it is done in heaven – completely, willingly and joyfully – each one of us living, day by day, to please you in all that we say and do.

To give us today all that we need to live in this world in a way that brings honour to your name.

By your Holy Spirit, to stir and enable us to be as amazingly forgiving of others as you have been of us. Cause a readiness to forgive others to be the hallmark of your people and of each one of us individually.

We are weak and easily led astray by the evil one, by others, as well as by our own passions and desires. Stir us to watch and pray and to walk humbly with you, and spare us from being overwhelmed by situations we cannot handle.

Keep us from evil thinking, evil speaking and evil deeds. Deliver us from the evil one and those under the evil one. Spare us from those who hate you; who would remove you and your Son from the throne and put something or someone else on your throne, and who would suppress your truth or oppress your people.

For yours alone is the kingdom; all power and authority are rightfully yours, and all glory belongs to you alone.

Lord God, heavenly Father, we plead with you to hear our prayers for the honour and glory of your name.

Amen

Postscript

The Lord's Prayer is like a lion. I long that it might be set free from being confined to the cage of formal religion, in which it has been kept chained for far too long. Under the hand of the Lord God, it can then fulfil its divine purpose.

Individually, it will open our eyes to see a far greater vision of the kingdom of God. It will change the focus of our thinking, our relationships with one another and the purposes to which we devote our lives.

Locally, it will touch our families and workplaces, shape our churches, and over the years encourage us to play our part in making the world around us as God would have it be.

Nationally and internationally, in these few memorable words are the seeds of liberty and justice, trust and true fellowship of families, and of families of peoples, all founded on a common submission to the Lord God, our heavenly Father.

The Lord's Prayer is so much more than a gentle murmur. It is a prayer to change the world – beginning with those who pray it.

Under God's New Covenant, his ancient promise to Solomon has world-wide application:

'If my people, who are called by my name, will humble themselves, and pray, and seek my face and turn from their ungodly ways; then I will hear from heaven, and will forgive their sin and heal their land.'
2 Chronicles 7:14

Acknowledgement

Many years back Dr J. I. Packer wrote a series of short articles on the Lord's Prayer for inclusion in church magazines. It was this series that first began to open my eyes to the richness, breadth and depth of this most wonderful of prayers. I gladly and gratefully acknowledge that all that follows has sprung from those early seeds.

A Greater Acknowledgement

The personal setting of this book

A Praying Teacher, a Crystal Diode and Winter Wheat
A twelve year old lad, headphones on, oblivious to the world, sprawled out at the top of the stairs, right in the way – fiddling with a very simple radio receiver; a crystal set. Will it work? Only if he can get the little wire to touch on the crystal at such a point that it makes a one way electrical gateway; a diode. He tried this way and that, between times adjusting the tuning condenser to search for the different radio stations. Nothing. Then, suddenly, he hit the spot. The little wire, known as the cat's whisker, was now making contact with a 'sweet spot' and the whole device sprang to life.

A live broadcast filled my headphones and ears. Was it music? Was it the news, the weather or a discussion? No, it was none of these. It was a preacher preaching!

Was it the preaching or the fact that the little, home-built radio set worked? I don't know. But I listened right to the end and, when it finished, determined that I wanted to hear more. The preacher's talks were being relayed by telephone line to a local church, and I asked my Dad to take me to hear him. No razzmatazz, no great build up, nothing visual, just a song and a talk. But through it the Lord God spoke as clearly as any voice, 'John, it is you I want.' I nudged my Dad but he was quite unmoved and, in talking with the minister of the church we attended as a family, he was assured, 'Don't worry, of course he'll soon get over it.' I would have done, but for Miss Gibbs, a teacher at school who taught both English and what was known in those far off days as 'Scripture'. With hindsight, that lady plainly not only taught her youngsters but coveted them for the Lord and prayed for them. It was Miss Gibbs who recognised that the Lord God had begun a work in my life and patiently encouraged me to begin to read the New Testament.

The little seed of faith began to grow, springing up like wheat sown in the mild autumn weather. However, as a family, we moved away very soon after that and the next ten years proved to be a very severe spiritual winter, with little or no Christian fellowship or encouragement. Spiritual life withered away, like the wheat in winter; yellowed and to all appearances dead and finished. Until, that is, a spiritual springtime in my twenties saw faith rekindled and the winter-sown wheat vigorously sprouting.

It was the second, tiny 'chance happening' under the hand of God. David, a friend in the local actors' club, offered me a lift.

He was going to visit a church in 'West Ken', which I took to be a few miles down the road in Kent. It wasn't, it was in Kensington – yet here was the vital Christianity I hadn't encountered since a young schoolboy.

After a while, I was even willing to heed a long-known, nagging suspicion that the Lord God would have me 'turn my collar round' – to become a Christian minister. It culminated in a prayer that you won't find in any prayer book, 'O.K. Lord, you win.' My employer's reaction astonished me, 'But of course,' as did my landlady's, 'Yes, it is about time you stopped messing about.'

I have had the privilege of marrying, bringing up a family and working for many years among some wonderful people in both city and rural ministry.

Day by day I remain thrilled and amazed by the gracious dealing, mercy and love of the Lord God, and just so grateful for his kindness, mercy and patience with such a difficult and wayward son. Yet an adopted son I find myself to be, and one rescued and redeemed by the cross of his Son. In the apostle Paul's words, I gladly confess, 'I live by faith in the Son of God who loved me and gave himself for me.' Of course, 'He'll soon get over it.' But, by the grace of the Lord God, I haven't yet, and that was said over sixty years ago!

As you can see, it is the story of God's gracious dealing with a rebellious and unwilling child and could well be summed up as it began – 'saved by a cat's whisker'.

It is in this setting of great thankfulness to my heavenly Father, that the phrases of the Lord's Prayer have become such a precious spur to worship, and a guide and compass for life.

The Lord's Prayer really applied to each part of our lives, is a prayer to change each one of us, and to change our churches, our society and our world – for the honour of the Lord God, our heavenly Father.

The Author and our Other Publications

The Author

Born in Great Malvern, Worcestershire, England, John Belham has a scientific background, but for most of his life has had the privilege of serving with some very wonderful people, first in suburban ministry, then as Rector of a group of country parishes, and more recently assisting with city ministry. Married with four grown-up children, he delights in the Lord God – his word, his people and his creation.

Exploring and Applying the Lord's Prayer

The e-book edition, *Exploring and Applying the Lord's Prayer, A Prayer to Change the World*, published by Parva Press in 2021. ISBN 978-0-9537489-1-4

Lord, teach us to pray . . . the Lord's Prayer explored and applied, published by Parva Press in 2000 (Paperback 125 pages). ISBN 0-9537489-0-1

This first edition has illustrations and more references to British history. The remaining copies of this edition are offered on the website below.

For further details and to hear the accompanying podcasts, visit https://www.lords-prayer.co.uk or search online 'Exploring and applying the Lord's Prayer'.

(An edition, published in 2018 by Grace and Truth Publications, under the title, *To Change the World for Good . . . Exploring and Applying the Lord's Prayer* is no longer widely available.)

Exploring and Applying the Parables of Jesus found in the Gospel of Luke

For those who have ears to hear, the parables of Jesus speak as sharply and relevantly today as they did 2,000 years ago. If you are willing to be stirred and challenged – as the first hearers were – read this book. The pages invite you to an exploration of each parable, pinpointing its encouragements and warnings, and offering questions for personal reflection or group discussion.

The details: *Exploring and Applying the Parables of Jesus found in the Gospel of Luke* Parva Press, Published 2022, ISBN 978-0-9537489-2-1, 403pages. Available from Amazon and booksellers worldwide.
Also published as an Ebook ISBN 978-0-9537489-3-8

For further details, reviews, a colour picture of the cover and sample chapters, search 'Exploring and applying the parables' or go to www.parables.org.uk

OUR OTHER PUBLICATIONS · 139

Exploring and Applying the Parables of Jesus found in the Gospel of Luke

John Belham

The cover images are from an overland expedition to the Middle East and Jerusalem, undertaken by a group of students in 1964. Top row: a country lane near Nazareth; one of us on a borrowed, shepherd's donkey; bottom row: a typical oil lamp; the sea of Galilee – around whose shores and surrounding hills so much of the ministry of Jesus took place.

www.ingramcontent.com/pod-product-compliance
Lightning Source LLC
Chambersburg PA
CBHW072047290426
44110CB00014B/1585